AMAZING IRV'S
Handbook of Everyday Magic

Library of Congress Control Number: 2001094932

ISBN: 1-931686-01-7

Printed in Singapore

Typeset in Bulldog, Clarendon, and Tiki Magic

Designed by Frances J. Soo Ping Chow
Illustrations by Lo Cole

Distributed in North America by Chronicle Books
85 Second Street
San Francisco, CA 94105

10 9 8 7 6 5 4 3 2 1

Quirk Books
215 Church Street
Philadelphia, PA 19106
www.quirkbooks.com

Introduction

MAGIC EVERYDAY, EVERYWHERE, ANYTIME

As every true magician knows, a master conjurer can make magic happen anytime, anyplace—once he or she has mastered the essentials. *Amazing Irv's Handbook of Everyday Magic* is the perfect place to begin to learn the basic techniques and principles that apply magic to the situations of daily life, at home, at work, and every place in between. With just a few mundane, everyday objects at hand, you'll be amazing your coworkers, friends, family, and fellow commuters in no time flat.

The Basics

This book will not teach you how to cure the terminally ill or to retire at age 30. But it will let you in on all sorts of small-scale tricks of magic that are often very easy to achieve—once you know how.

Seemingly random acts of magic require at least some measure of the three basic components of every trick: **preparation**, **secrecy**, and **misdirection**. These elements are guided by the Five Golden Rules of Magic:

Rule #1. Explore Alternatives

Rule #2. Make Preparations

Rule #3. Practice

Rule #4. Practice

Rule #5. Practice

Everyday Magic

If you've ever wished you could make yourself levitate, if you've ever wondered, "What's he/she *really* thinking?" or if you've ever just really wanted to be the life of the party or to entertain your seat companion on an airplane, this is the essential handbook you've been looking for. The chapters that follow will guide you to all the best deceptions and sleights-of-hand that can be accomplished with little preparation and minimal props.

"Magic Begins at Home" highlights tricks you can master with basic household items such as laundry line, ordinary dental floss, and a television remote. "Magic Goes to Work" features tricks based on simple office supplies, including pencils, paper clips, rubber bands, and the company directory. "Magic on the Go" transforms airsickness bags, newspapers, and cell phones into magic props for planes, trains, and automobiles. "Magic on the Town" teaches you tricks for restaurants, bars, and street corners using such unassuming items as napkins, matchboxes, sugar packets, and money.

Magic is where you make it. All you need is the will to make it happen . . . along with some inspiration, improvisation, and a few good paper clips!

Note: In the following pages, the "What You'll Need" sections list the objects necessary for doing the tricks, but if you don't have those *exact* items on hand, try some magical improvisation! (For example, try using different denomination coins or bills—or even different currency entirely—for those tricks that require money.)

Chapter 1

MAGIC BEGINS AT HOME

The family that plays together, stays together. That's why we've compiled a series of fun-filled everyday magic tricks that just about anyone can do easily, in the comfort of their own home. In fact, you could even do these tricks in someone else's home (provided you're not breaking and entering).

There are so many uses for magic around the house—just think about what it can do for you: You can entertain an angry father who's about to administer your punishment (see How to Make Yourself Levitate). You can win the heart of a tired mother who wants nothing more than an extra hour in the day (see How to Make Time Stand Still). You can distract the kids who want nothing more than macaroni and cheese for dinner—again (see How to Make Canned Spinach Surprise).

By using everyday magic at home, you can transform even the most mundane chores into exciting magical events (see How to Magically Mend a Clothesline and How to Turn Two Pieces of Dental Floss into One).

There's no end to the magic you can spread around your house. And by obeying the cardinal rule of magic—**never perform a trick twice in a row**—you'll soon have your entire family begging you to let them in on the secrets behind your magical powers.

How to Be a
Crayon Psychic

Picture this: You're about to serve dessert to your hungry horde, and your kids meantime have already covered the entire tablecloth with crayon drawings. The only place left to draw another stick figure or squiggle-dragon is on the napkins—which are linen and expensive to replace. Now you need to take the crayons away *and* keep the little monsters entertained! This trick will instantly widen their eyes in wonder. (*Warning:* After they see it, your greatest challenge will be finding another way to entertain them so they'll stop asking you to do the crayon trick again.)

What They See

You hand your small friend a box of crayons and turn your back. You ask him to think of one of the colors and remove the appropriate crayon from the box. You place both of your hands behind your back, then ask the child to place the chosen crayon in your hand. By merely holding the crayon, and without peeking, you are able to tell him the color he selected.

What You'll Need

A box of crayons

Fig. A. Place both of your hands behind your back and ask the child to place the chosen crayon in one of your hands.

Fig. B. Use your thumbnail to scrape enough colored wax to leave a small amount under your nail, then switch the crayon into your other hand.

Fig. C. Place your hand on your forehead as though you are concentrating on the chosen crayon.

Fig. D. Take a peek at your thumbnail and reveal the color!

What You'll Do

This trick does not take much time to master and can be performed nearly anywhere.

1. As above, ask a child to choose a crayon from the box.
2. Place both of your hands behind your back.
3. Ask the child to put the chosen crayon in one of your hands. (Fig. A)
4. With your hands still behind your back, use your thumbnail to scrape the crayon. Scrape enough to leave a small amount of wax under your nail, then switch the crayon into your other hand. (Fig. B)
5. Now bring your empty hand forward and place it on your forehead as though you are concentrating on his choice. (Fig. C)
6. Now take a peek at your thumbnail and reveal the color. (Fig. D)

A simple trick—but one that'll have them *convinced* of your psychic powers!

An Optional Add-on

If you want to extend this basic trick a step further, you can now tell the child that you have the power to make the crayon you're holding write any color they choose. If you are holding a red crayon and the child says he wants the crayon to write blue, simply write the word *blue* on the paper. You're sure to get a chuckle out of this little add-on!

How to Perform
Paperback Magic

Didn't you always hate those people who could quote Chaucer, Shakespeare, and Milton—all at the drop of a hat? How did they remember that stuff? Didn't they have anything better to do with their time? And really, deep down, didn't you want to be just like them? With the secrets of paperback magic you *can* be just like them, only without the pretentiousness. Impress your neighbors, belittle your spouse, or trick your kids during reading hour with your extraordinary literary prowess, as you recite from the canon of Grisham, Christie, and Steel!

What They See

You have selected a couple of random paperback books from your bookshelf and placed them on the table. You tell your neighbor that you've committed every word of each book to memory. To prove it, you ask your neighbor to pick up any one of the books and hand it to you. You flip through the pages until your neighbor says "stop." You turn your head away and ask your neighbor to look at the top line of the page he stopped at, and to remember it. There is no way that you could possibly know the chosen line, but—amazingly—you pronounce the line exactly as it appears on the page.

What You'll Need

One or two paperbacks

A pencil

Some preparation time (about 20 minutes for a 200-page book)

What You'll Do

This trick requires that you "gimmick" a paperback book, or several if you choose.

1. Before your neighbor arrives, take a pencil and write the first line that appears on every left-hand page on the top of every right-hand page.

2. Now you're ready to begin. Make sure that the back cover of the book faces your neighbor.

3. Using your thumb at the top corner, flip through the pages, starting from the back of the book. (Beginning from the back of the book and flipping through the top corners will allow you to conceal your writing on the right-hand pages.) If you hold the book at about arm's length, right in front of your neighbor, this will be even more convincing.

4. When your neighbor says "stop," let him read the top line on the left-hand page and remember it.

5. While he reads the line, merely take a peek at the right-hand page to get your sentence. Then quickly turn your head away so that your neighbor thinks there is no possible way that you could have been looking.

6. Close the book.

7. Pronounce the chosen line with your most pompous accent.

Note: The line doesn't absolutely need to be given word for word—in fact, it's even more convincing when you give them just the gist of the line, as if it were coming to you through psychic waves.

How to Make
Dishwashing Magic

Are you always stuck as the designated dishwasher? Here's a sure-fire way to get out of it. Bet your brother or sister (or mother or father or dinner guests) that you have the power of *anti-dis-a-pepper-and-magnetism*. If they know what you're talking about, then you're well on your way. If they don't, well, just tell them that you hate pepper and pepper hates you. Then bet them that if you can prove it, they have to do the dishes!

What They See

After you've soaped up a dish or two, you invite everyone to gather around as you show off your powers of magnetic repulsion. You toss your black pepper shaker into the air with aplomb, deftly catch it, then proceed to sprinkle several shakes into a nearby water glass. Suddenly, you raise your index finger into the air, then plunge it into the water's depths. Amazingly, the pepper grains quickly move to the walls of the glass as if by magnetic repulsion.

What You'll Need

A pepper shaker

Some dishwashing liquid (any brand will do)

A glass of water (any size will do)

What You'll Do

1. Before inviting your audience into the kitchen, coat one of your index fingers with dishwashing liquid.

2. Now, call in your spectators.

3. Using your opposite hand, toss and catch the shaker, then sprinkle the pepper into the glass of water until it completely covers the surface of the water.

4. Wiggle your index finger in the air, then dip the tip of it into the glass of water. The pepper will naturally flow away from your finger, and toward the walls of the glass.

You've just performed a feat even Merlin would be proud of!

How to Make
a Ball Dance

There you are, minding your own business, when that special someone asks you to dance in the living room. Unfortunately—for your spouse or partner—your ability to move through space is significantly hindered by your two left feet. How do you avoid embarrassment without hurting that special someone's feelings? Instead of tripping all over the light fantastic, use this dancing ball trick to show the world another way to defy gravity. Make a small ball levitate—no strings attached!

What They See

You rest a small ball atop a drinking glass. With a flourish, you cover the ball with a cloth or table napkin. Amazingly, as you hold only the top two corners of the cloth, the ball defies gravity. It begins to move under the cloth and floats high above the table!

What You'll Need

A table napkin measuring approximately 20 inches square

A 3-inch Styrofoam ball (available at your local crafts shop)

A metal clothes hanger

A drinking glass (smaller than 3 inches in diameter)

A tube of lipstick (or other cylindrical object)

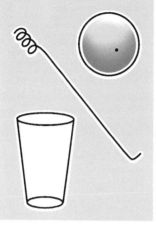

Fig. A. Your gimmicks include a Styrofoam ball, a metal hanger with one end coiled, and a drinking glass.

Fig. B. Hold the napkin by opposite corners, with the hanger running between the thumb and index finger of each hand.

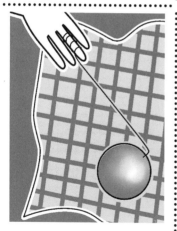

Fig. C. Under cover of the napkin, slip your middle finger into the coil, and fit the other end of the hanger into the small hole in the ball.

Fig. D. Use the hanger to control the ball and make it move under the napkin!

What You'll Do

This trick will require a small amount of preparation and a few gimmicked props. (Fig. A) Steps 1–6 should be done before you face your audience.

1. Straighten the metal hanger and cut it to about 16 inches.

2. Uncoil the hooked end and bend one end, about $\frac{1}{2}$ inch, at a 90-degree angle.

3. Wrap the other end around a lipstick, or other cylindrical object that size; remove the cylinder to create a coil.

4. Using the angled end of the hanger, create a small hole on the surface of the Styrofoam ball.

5. Now your gimmicks are ready to use: Set your ball atop the drinking glass. The hole should be facing you.

6. As you call in your audience, cover the hanger with the napkin.

7. With the hanger still hidden under the napkin, pick up the napkin and hanger as one, and place the napkin so that one flap covers the ball. You should hold the napkin by opposite corners, with the hanger running between the thumb and index finger of each hand. (Fig. B)

8. Secretly slipping your middle finger into the coiled end of the hanger, fit the other end of the hanger into the small hole in the ball. (Fig. C) (Practice this move first using your right middle finger and then your left middle finger to see which feels most comfortable for you.)

9. Using the hanger to control the ball, you can now manipulate the ball and cause it to move beneath the napkin. (Fig. D)

Your audience is sure to get a rise out of this gravity-defying phenomenon!

How to Conduct
Candy Teleportation

Beam me up Scotty . . . or over, anyway. What better way to take your kids away from the tube or those three obsessive "W's" than with a little futuristic magic? For now—because of technological limitations—the everyday magician can only perform teleportation with two similar objects, such as two different-flavored hard candies. But those objects can be anything as long as they fit in the palm of your hand (like two different-colored grapes) and/or can leap small houses with a single bound (like two different-colored super balls), and/or are more powerful than a localized headache (like an aspirin and a vitamin).

What They See

You wrap a yellow candy in a light-colored handkerchief and tuck them into a wide-mouthed drinking glass. You repeat this with a green candy, wrapping it in a dark cloth. You have your spectator press a button on your shirt. (You tell them that this is your teleportation activation button.) After they press your button, have them unwrap the candies. The two candies have magically changed places!

What You'll Need

Two wide-mouthed drinking glasses

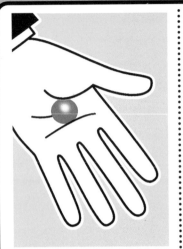

Fig A. Hide one of the duplicate candies in the palm of your hand.

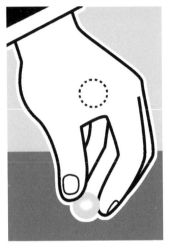

Fig. B. Using the same hand, pick up the contrasting candy with your fingertips.

Fig. C. Simultaneously cover the candy with a coordinating handkerchief and switch the palmed candy with the one in your fingertips.

Fig. D. Place the wrapped candy into a glass.

Three pieces of standard-size hard candy. Two of the candies must be the same color and the other should contrast.

Two handkerchiefs (in colors that coordinate with the colors of the two different-colored candies; e.g., a white cloth for the yellow candy, a black cloth for the green one)

What You'll Do

1. Hide one of the duplicate candies in the palm of your hand. (Fig. A)
2. With the same hand, pick up the contrasting candy with your fingertips. (Fig. B)
3. Simultaneously cover this candy with a coordinating handkerchief and switch the palmed candy with the one in your fingertips. (Fig. C) (Now you're palming the candy you just picked up.) The motion of wrapping the hankie around the candy serves as misdirection.
4. Place the wrapped candy into a glass. (Fig. D)
5. Repeat the process: Pick up the third candy with your fingertips, switch it with the palmed candy, wrap it in the second handkerchief, and place them in the second glass.
6. You are now left with a palmed candy in your hand, which you slip into your pocket while the spectator presses your "teleportation" button.
7. Your spectator unwraps the handkerchiefs to reveal that the candies have switched places!

Spock and Scotty would be proud of your abilities to teleport!

How to Vanish
a CD

Do Internet CDs fill your mailbox? Does your daughter's heavy-metal music get you down? Has your son figured out how to get around your parental control software and burn unmentionable sites with your CD-R? If so, this trick is for you! Say goodbye to all those troublesome disks for good with this remarkable vanishing CD trick.

What They See

You are holding an ordinary CD between your hands. You cover it with a handkerchief or napkin. Then, tossing the covered CD high into the air, the handkerchief comes fluttering down—but the CD has completely vanished!

What You'll Need

A CD that you'll never use

A drill

A 24-inch piece of elastic or linked rubber bands

A safety pin

A jacket

A handkerchief

What You'll Do

For hundreds of years, magicians have been vanishing small objects with the aid of a simple device called a pull. Unscrupulous gamblers also used this gimmick. A pull is merely a piece of elastic that is attached with a safety pin to the inside of a jacket. (In this case, the elastic has a CD fastened to its other end.)

1. Using a fine drill, drill a small hole at the edge of your CD.

2. Tie a 24-inch piece of elastic to the CD. If you don't have a piece of elastic, you can string together some heavy-duty rubber bands.

3. Pin the other end of the elastic to the inside top of your jacket, right between your shoulders. The elastic should be adjusted so that the CD hangs down just to the bottom of your jacket but does not protrude below the hem. (Fig. A)

4. Right before you perform the vanish, get ready by reaching your left hand behind you and bringing the CD to the front, holding it between your two hands. The elastic line should be running parallel to your left arm, out of sight. Be careful not to expose it. With the tension now on the elastic, if you should let go, your CD would shoot behind your jacket.

5. Now you are ready to perform your little miracle. (Here is where practice and timing come in.) Cover the CD with the handkerchief, placing your hands on the outside edges of the cloth and holding the handkerchief and CD as one. (Fig. B)

Fig. A. Pin the elastic to the inside of your jacket, so that the CD hangs down to (but not below) the hem.

Fig. B. The elastic line is now running parallel to your left arm. With the CD covered, hold the CD and cloth as one.

Fig. C. As your upper body turns, bring your arms down to waist level and let go of the CD, but keep hold of the handkerchief.

Fig. D. Throw your arms and the handkerchief high into the air, and look upward to distract your audience.

6. Turn at the hips a quarter turn to your left. As the upper part of your body is turning, bring your arms down to waist level and secretly let go of the CD, allowing it to slip from your fingertips but keeping hold of the handkerchief. (Fig. C)

7. Just as the CD is secretly leaving the handkerchief, throw your arms and the handkerchief high into the air. This all should be done in one fluid motion. As your arms go up, you must look upward as you follow the path of the tossed handkerchief. (Fig. D)

8. When the handkerchief comes floating down, catch it out of the air and show it to be empty. The CD has completely vanished!

Now take a bow to thunderous applause. With some practice in front of a mirror, you should be an instant maven.

How to Make Time Stand Still

So you say you want to stop time, eh? You've just been proposed to, you've just taken a bite of the most scrumptious barbequed T-bone you've ever tasted, you've just met a girl named "Maria" (you know, the most beautiful sound you've ever heard), and you want to remember this moment for the rest of your life! What better way to seize the moment than to stop time and make the minute last for two?

What They See

You borrow a watch from a friend and hold it in the palm of your hand. You announce to your audience: "I am now going to demonstrate my psychokinetic abilities by causing the second hand on your watch to stop." As you gaze at the watch, the second hand freezes in time. Your audience is awed by your powers. Now, at your command, the second hand begins ticking once again. You are in full control at all times.

What You'll Need

- A small, rare earth magnet, about the size of a baby aspirin (These can be purchased at www.phillymagic.com or at a science supply store, for about two dollars.)
- A plain ring (Any kind of ring will work, and the material does not matter.)

What You'll Do

1. Slip the magnet under the palm side of your ring, preferably one worn on your ring finger.

2. When you place the watch in your hand, make sure that the back of the watch is directly above your ring.

3. Move your finger slightly upward, and therefore in contact with the back of the watch, and the magnet will cause the second hand to stop.

4. When your finger is slightly lowered, time moves on.

Tip: This may not work on some watches (e.g., any non-battery-operated watch). If this is the case, explain to your audience that your psychic abilities are drained today and move on to another trick.

Caution: It is important that you do not leave a watch exposed to the magnet for extended periods of time. Exposure to the magnet for about one minute will not harm the watch, but anything longer than that will possibly do some damage.

How to Make
Canned Spinach Surprise

Can't get your kids to eat their spinach? Bet the little whippersnappers that if you can turn a can of peaches into a can of spinach, they've got to eat every bite of the bitter green. Nothing says loving like the old spinach can/peach can switcheroo. This truly transforming trick will have them begging for more.

What They See

You lower a can of peaches into a paper bag. With a few magic words and a tap from your magic spatula, you remove the can from the bag and—voilà!—it's turned into a can of spinach!

Your observers, of course, assume that the can of peaches is still in the bag and that you have merely made a switch. But now you pick up the bag, crumble it into a ball, and throw it over your shoulder. The peaches have disappeared!

What You'll Need

A can of spinach (or other unappealing canned vegetables)

A can of peaches (the same size as the spinach can)

A brown paper bag large enough to conceal the can of spinach

Scotch tape

Scissors or a razor blade

Fig. A. Place the peaches label over the spinach label and secure it with a small piece of tape.

Fig. B. Show the children the can of "peaches," making sure that the taped seam is concealed.

Fig. C. As you lower the can into the bag, tear the peaches label with your index finger.

Fig. D. Pull the can out of the bag. It's morphed into a can of spinach!

What You'll Do

This trick requires a small amount of prepping.

1. Carefully remove the label from a can of peaches, keeping it intact.
    (**Tip:** You can use a razor blade to cut the label in an inconspicuous area, such as on a preexisting seam.)

2. Carefully place the peaches label over the label on a can of spinach, and secure it with a small piece of scotch tape. (Fig. A) Be sure not to allow the tape to come in contact with the spinach label.

3. Now you're ready to perform your magic: Show the children the can of "peaches," making sure to hold the can so that the taped seam is concealed. (Fig. B)

4. As you lower the can into the bag, use your index finger to tear off the peaches label and allow it to fall to the bottom of the bag. (Fig. C)

5. Pull the can out of the bag, revealing it now as a can of delicious, nutritious spinach. (Fig. D)

6. Get rid of your evidence by crumbling the bag and throwing it over your shoulder.

Tip: It's a good idea to draw your spectators' attention away from the bag you just discarded. Quickly move on to another trick, or tell a favorite joke to distract them.

How to Magnetize Your Hand

Can't sink a putt, hit a pitch, or serve a ball even when you're in your own backyard? With this amazing magnetic hand trick, you can psyche out opponents, stun a pitcher, and scare your neighbors with your "magnetic personality." Watch your enemies crumble—or at least miss the next shot—as you demonstrate your ability to hold up just about anything with your powerful magnetic hand. (*Warning:* As long as you can hold it in your hand, you can "magnetize" it, so . . . be careful what you use.)

What They See

You grasp a simple, oblong object—anything from a yardstick, to a pencil, to a pair of scissors, to a baseball bat—in your hand. You slowly open your hand and, remarkably, the object stays magnetized to your palm!

What You'll Need

Any oblong object (see above)

What You'll Do

1. Place the object in your hand and close your fist around it. The object should be held vertically, and the back of your hand should be facing your audience. (Fig. A)

Fig. A. Place the object in your hand and close your fist around it so that the back of your hand is facing your audience.

Fig. B. Grab your wrist with your opposite hand and squeeze it.

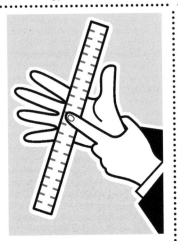

Fig. C. To hold the object in place, extend the index finger of the hand that's grasping your wrist.

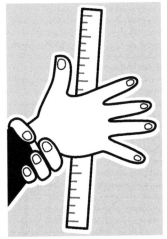

Fig. D. Slowly open your hand and extend your fingers.

2. Grab your wrist with your opposite hand and squeeze it. (Fig. B) Heighten the effect by making grunting noises as you squeeze.

3. Extend the index finger of the hand that's grasping your wrist, allowing it to hold the object in place. Your missing index finger will not even be noticed. (Fig. C)

4. Slowly open your opposite hand and extend your fingers. The object will appear to be stuck to your hand! (Fig. D)

5. Close your hand back into a fist, then hand a spectator the object and allow him to try.

A More Advanced Version

This more advanced version will require just a bit more practice.

What They See

You hold a cane in front of you in your two hands. As you open your hands, extending your fingers, it will appear as though the cane has become magnetized to your hands.

What You'll Need

A wooden walking cane with a hooked handle

What You'll Do

1. Grasp the cane in both hands and hold it horizontally in front of your body, with your palms facing away from your body.

2. As you adjust your two hands on the cane, slide your left hand along the shaft until it reaches the balancing point—the point where, when you open your hand, the cane stays attached. (**Tip:** Finding the balancing point of the cane will take some practice and may vary depending on the size and weight of the cane.)

3. The cane now is resting on the heel of your left palm.

4. Open the fingers of your left hand.

5. Slowly slide away your right hand, leaving the cane attached to your palm.

How to Turn
Two Pieces of Dental Floss
into One

We all floss every day, right? At least that's what we tell the dentist. And everybody knows how to make one piece of dental floss into two—just floss a little harder between those two teeth that the retainer just couldn't fix. But not everyone knows how to make two pieces of dental floss into one . . . until now. Five out of five dentists surveyed say that one piece of floss works better than two, and that the "two-pieces-of-floss-into-one" trick is a great way to entertain the kids while they clean their teeth.

What They See

You show your kids the two pieces of floss, each one approximately 12 inches long. You place the two top ends into your mouth, and when you take them out, the two pieces have magically become one!

What You'll Need

One piece of floss (waxed or unwaxed) about 24 inches long

One piece of floss about 3 inches long

What You'll Do

1. Prepare in advance by folding the long piece of floss in half.

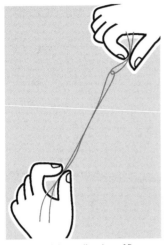

Fig. A. Thread the smaller piece of floss around the center of the longer piece.

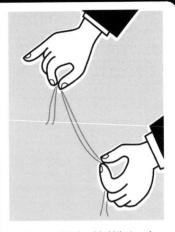

Fig. B. In your right hand, hold the two pieces together so that the 3-inch ends dangle; in your left hand, hold the two ends of the longer piece, leaving about 3 inches dangling.

Fig. C. Beginning with the combined floss ends in your right hand, place the floss into your mouth.

Fig. D. Using your tongue to hold the U piece in place, pull out the single long piece with a flourish!

2. Thread the 3-inch piece of floss around the center of the 24-inch floss, forming a U shape. (Fig. A)

3. Now you're ready for your audience. Hold the two pieces of floss together between your right thumb and your right index and middle fingers, so that the 3-inch floss ends dangle to the side. (This will conceal the interlocking floss pieces as you place the floss into your mouth.) At the same time, hold the two ends of the longer floss between your left thumb and left index and middle fingers, leaving about 3 inches to dangle at the floss ends. (Fig. B)

4. Now, beginning with the floss ends in your right hand, place the floss into your mouth. (Fig. C)

5. Once you have about 2 inches of the floss in your mouth, use your tongue to hold the 3-inch U piece in place, and pull out the single piece of floss with a flourish. (Fig. D)

Presto! The two pieces have magically become one!

Tip: This illusion happens very quickly and does not take much practice, though you should not perform any magic without at least a few practice runs.

How to Perform
Tele(vision) Kinesis

Your spouse has decided to throw a boring cocktail party on the same night as the final episode of your favorite Reality Show. But meanwhile, you're missing the last episode of *Sports Star/Rock Star Survivor!* Who will win the final challenge? Michael Jordan or Yanni? You know everyone will be talking about it tomorrow at the water cooler, and you've just got to catch it. How to subtly suggest that you all cut the banter and turn on the big-screen TV? This trick should do the trick . . .

What They See
You start off with a little bit of patter: "Did you know that scientists are studying how the powers of the mind work? Well, I'd like to demonstrate for you what human powers can do. If we all concentrate together, maybe we can even make that TV turn on with our minds!" You wiggle your fingers and—eureka!—the TV flicks on!

What You'll Need
   A remote control
   A trusted assistant

What You'll Do

1. You will need to enlist the help of an assistant to perform this feat. Be sure that this is someone who can be trusted not to divulge the trick. This person should have excellent eyesight and good hand-eye coordination.

2. Have your accomplice procure the TV remote control.

3. Now, out of site of your audience, work out your signals: Arrange with your accomplice so that whenever you wiggle your fingers at the TV, she will turn it on.

4. Whenever you raise or lower your hand, your accomplice will change the volume accordingly.

5. Whenever you snap your fingers, your accomplice will cause the channels to change.

6. As above, begin your patter, then proceed to astonish your audience. They'll be so entranced, they won't even notice it when you settle in to watch your program.

Note: For this trick, presentation is everything. Perform it with your own special brand of showmanship! Get crazy. (The more exuberant, the better.)

How to Make Yourself Levitate

You didn't listen when the neighbors told you *not* to take the kids to the new fantasy movie—now they won't get out from under the covers of your bed. Well, there's only one way to allay their fears. With this nifty trick, you can prove to your kids that you have more magical powers than the Wicked Witch of the West.

What They See

You are standing directly in front of your kids. You slowly raise your arms out to your sides as your feet lift off the floor. Your feet come several inches off the ground, and now you seem to be rising in the air, without any apparatus, with no strings attached!

What You'll Need

Just the right amount of showmanship

What You'll Do

This illusion is best performed one on one. Angles are very important here: What actually happens is that you are creating an illusion of rising off the floor when in fact one foot comes off the floor about 4 inches and the other is on tiptoe. This feat is best performed while wearing a comfortable pair of thick-soled sneakers.

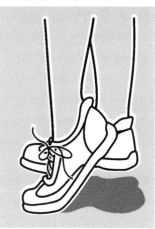

Fig. A. As you slowly lift your right foot, which remains straight, bring your left foot into a tiptoe position.

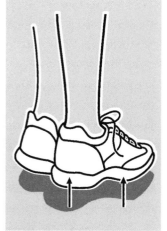

Fig. B. To your spectator, both feet appear to come off the ground.

Fig. C. As you lift your foot, spread your arms out to your sides to enhance the illusion.

1. Stand facing your spectator in a slightly angled position—so that your right leg is pointing slightly toward your spectators' right shoulder—with your arms at your sides and your feet together.

2. Keep your right leg stiff and straight.

3. Now shift your weight to your left foot as you slowly lift your right foot, which remains parallel to the floor at all times.

4. At the same time, your left foot goes into a tiptoe position. (Fig. A) To your spectator's eye, both feet appear to be levitating, as your heels come into alignment. (Fig. B)

5. As you are lifting, slowly bring your arms out to your sides to help you retain "balance" and add to the illusion. (Fig. C)

A truly uplifting experience!

How to Magically Mend a Clothesline

If you always leave your laundry for someone else to do, the least you can do is set up a clothesline, right? That way, your clothes will retain that natural outdoors aroma—unless of course you live in the big city, in which case your clothes will retain that not-so-fresh aroma. Either way, a clothesline is an easy way to lend a hand. You still won't have to do your laundry. All you'll have to do is mend the line once in a while . . .

What They See

As your spouse and/or family look on, you take a pair of scissors and cut the clothesline in two. Calmly, you assure them that you can fix the line. You tie the cut pieces back together in a knot, but within seconds you slip the knot and the two pieces have become one again!

What You'll Need

A 3-foot-long piece of clothesline

Scissors

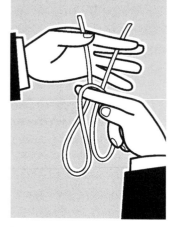

Fig. A. Holding both ends of the rope in one hand as shown, use your other hand to bring up the center loop.

Fig. B. As you bring your hand up, use your thumb and forefinger to create a small false loop in the rope that is being held between your opposite thumb and index finger.

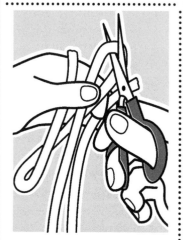

Fig. C. Cut the small false loop so that it appears to your audience that you've cut through the center of the rope.

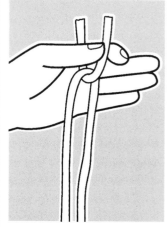

Fig. D. Allow the two ends of the rope to drop so that it looks as if the rope has been cut in two.

What You'll Do

Once you have your clothesline and scissors, you're ready to perform.

1. Hold both ends of the rope in one hand, one end between your thumb and index finger and one end between your index and middle fingers, allowing the center of the rope to dangle.

2. With your other hand, bring the center loop up to be grasped by your opposite thumb. (Fig. A)

3. As your bring the center loop up, use your thumb and index finger to pinch the rope just below your opposite thumb and index finger, and quickly create a false loop by bringing up the pinched rope to be held by your opposite thumb. (Fig. B) (**Note:** As you bring up the false loop, it will cross the *real* center loop.)

4. Cut the small false loop that you have created. It will appear to your audience that you have cut the center of the rope. (Fig. C)

5. Allow the two ends of the rope closest to the tip of your index finger to drop. This will give the illusion that the rope has been cut in two. (Fig. D)

6. Now tie the two top ends of the rope together, forming a loose knot.

7. At this point you actually have a long piece of rope and a short piece of rope. The short piece of rope creates the knot, but it will appear as though you have tied two separate pieces of rope together. Clearly show the knot in the center of the rope.

8. Grab the knot, slide it off of the rope, and hand the knot to your spouse as a souvenir. You've magically healed the rope!

Chapter 2

MAGIC GOES TO WORK

Who likes to wake up at six A.M. and trudge off to work?

The dedicated worker-magician, that's who.

With these handy-dandy tricks, specially designed for the workplace, you're bound to be the first one in the office. Okay, so that's mainly because, for a few of these tricks, you'll have to get there early to prepare. But of course being the first one there means . . . that's right, the boss sees your commitment and gives you a promotion and a raise!

Okay, so there are no guarantees about the raise. But we will guarantee that, with the extraordinary magic tricks you perform, you'll be the talk of the office. (We provide no guarantees about what people will be saying about you—just know that they will be talking.) Wow your coworkers with some pocket tape recorder clairvoyance! Impress the office staff with your linking paper clip magic! Astound everyone in the company lunchroom with some banana split trickery!

If those tricks don't do the trick, try to liven up your monthly budget meetings with some quarterly earnings magic. Or, just pass some time in the coffee break room with a little company directory telepathy. And while everybody else is keeping busy, keep yourself *looking* busy at your desk with some snake-charm pencil tricks.

And the best part about bringing magic to the office? With so many tricks to brighten the day for you and your coworkers, it'll be five P.M. in no time!

How to Make
Rubber Bands Jump

You're stuck in an interminable company-wide meeting, listening to your blowhard boss hold forth on yet another Five-Year Plan. You've just finished reading the paper and lunch is still three hours away. That rubber band you've been playing with sure would look great sailing toward your boss's shiny forehead—but then, what would you do for work? Instead of killing your job prospects, why not kill a few hours for yourself and your co-workers with a little rubber band magic?

What They See

You pull a rubber band down to the base of your index and middle fingers. You close your hand into a fist. When you open your hand again, the rubber band has magically penetrated and traveled to your ring finger and pinkie.

What You'll Need

Two standard-size rubber bands

What You'll Do

1. Place one rubber band around your index and middle fingers, so that the extra length of the band rests against your palm. (Fig. A)

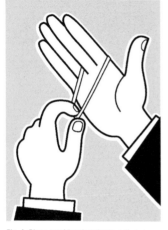

Fig. A. Place a rubber band around your index and middle fingers; the extra length of band should rest against your palm.

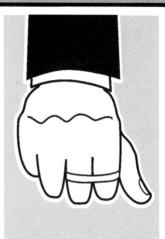

Fig. B. As you make a fist, secretly place all four fingertips into the band concealed in your fist.

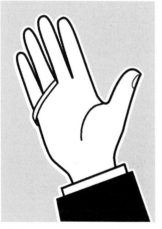

Fig. C. As you open your hand, the band will automatically jump to your pinkie and ring fingers!

Fig. A-1 (**A More Advanced Version**). Using a figure-8 pattern, interweave a second band around your four fingertips (excluding your thumb).

2. Now, make a fist, and secretly place all four fingertips into the band concealed in your fist. (Fig. B)

3. As you open your hand, the band will automatically jump to your ring and pinkie fingers. (Fig. C)

A More Advanced Version

This trick seems incredible enough, but your boss has just switched gears and has broken out his new marketing plan—something involving a fish and two sheep. Now that you have your coworkers' attention, it seems a shame not to give them something more . . .

What They See

Once again, you place a rubber band back on your index and middle fingers. Now, you interweave a second band around the tips of all your of fingers. You open and then close your hand once again, and—presto!— the first band has passed through the second band!

What You'll Do

1. As above, place a rubber band around your index and middle fingers, with the extra length resting against your palm.

2. Using a figure-8 pattern, interweave a second band around your four fingertips (excluding your thumb). (Fig. A-1)

3. Now, close your fingers into a fist. As you do so, quickly place your four

fingertips into the band concealed in your fist.

4. As you open your hand, the first band will jump automatically to your ring and pinkie fingers.

An Even <u>More</u> Advanced Version

Now, prepare your coworkers for your big finale.

What They See

You begin by interweaving one band on your four fingertips, making it impossible for any other bands to go onto your fingers. You then place a second band onto your middle finger and pull it right through the woven band. Your coworkers will not believe their eyes: The second band has penetrated the weave and rests at the base of your middle finger!

What You'll Do

1. Interweave one band around your four fingertips (excluding your thumb), creating a continuous figure 8.

2. Place your second band around your middle finger.

3. Spread your fingers slightly and, with your other hand, pull back sharply, toward your body, on the second band.

4. When the second band has reached the base of your fingers, clamp your fingers closed, trapping the second band in place. It will appear that the band has penetrated the woven band.

5. Now, with your palm facing the audience, allow one of your coworkers to pull the second band off. The figure-8 weave remains intact!

Note: If you're at home, you can also do this trick very effectively using ponytail holders.

Tip: Use contrasting colored rubber bands for a more colorful effect!

How to Make
Your Pocket Tape Recorder
Predict the Future

How many times have you killed 30 minutes in the office droning into your tape recorder, "Company memo . . . and please note that heretofore and henceforth all employees must change their socks at the top of the hour . . . blah, blah, blah"? Why not turn the tables on yourself and your coworkers? Punch up the afternoon with a little pocket tape recorder clairvoyance! It only takes a few minutes, but the joy it brings means double productivity for the rest of the day.

What They See

You select one of your coworkers as a volunteer and lead her through a few simple mathematical tasks. Now, you whip out your pocket tape recorder and place it on the table. You say, "Last night I had a dream. We were all together for a celebration. There were nine of us. Bill [use your coworkers' names], you were there, and so were you, Denise. I saw a clock, and its hands were glowing; it was five o'clock. I didn't want to forget this dream, so I grabbed my pocket tape recorder and this is what I recorded." The story you tell on the tape matches exactly your coworker's answers!

What You'll Need

A pocket tape recorder

What You'll Do

This trick is known as a mathematical and psychological "force." Although your coworker thinks she has free choice, she is guided to your pre-recorded prediction.

1. Before you gather your coworkers around, record a brief message. The text of the message appears in step 11, below.

2. Now, you must "force" a number. You do this by having your coworker choose a number between 1 and 10.

3. Have her multiply that number by 9.

4. If she has a two-digit number, have her add the two digits together.

5. Now have her subtract 5 from that number.

6. Ask her to figure out which letter of the alphabet her single-digit number corresponds to: For example, A corresponds to 1, B corresponds to 2, and so on. (Since you have forced the number 4, she should now be thinking of the letter D.)

7. Ask her to come up with a country that starts with the letter she is thinking of. (The country that comes to mind is Denmark 99 percent of the time.)

8. Have her concentrate on the second letter of the country she has mentally chosen. (This should be the letter E.)

9. Have her think of a mammal that begins with the second letter. (Once again, most people will choose an elephant.)

10. Have her concentrate on the color of the mammal she is thinking of. (Most elephants are gray—unless you're having a pink dream.)

11. Now it is time to play your pre-recorded prediction: "Denise, your plane has just arrived in Denmark. I see a clock on the wall. Its hands are glowing. It is nine o'clock. As you carry your five pieces of luggage to catch a cab, to your surprise standing in front of you are five gray elephants. But how strange—there are no gray elephants in Denmark!"

Mathematical Examples:

Spectator chooses to start with 2:	2 x 9 = 18	1 + 8 = 9	9 − 5 = 4	4 = D
Spectator chooses to start with 5:	5 x 9 = 45	4 + 5 = 9	9 − 5 = 4	4 = D
Spectator chooses to start with 7:	7 x 9 = 63	6 + 3 = 9	9 − 5 = 4	4 = D

How to Win Friends and Influence People

Everyone has a mentor or role model who contributed tremendously to their personal and professional growth—Gandhi, Bill Gates, Groucho Marx—the possibilities are many. But not everyone has the power to *tell you* who your mentor is! Now you do: With the powers of everyday magic, you'll deduce the most influential person in your coworkers' lives in less time than it takes to check your voicemail. (*Warning:* Remember to use this secret effect for entertainment purposes only. This is really strong magic!)

What They See

You have your coworker think of a person who was influential in his life. You hand him a pad of paper with the numbers 1 to 5 written down the left side. You ask your coworker to write his special person's name next to any one of the numbers, and to fill the other four spots with individuals in his life who were not as influential but still important. You take a quick glance at the piece of paper and then into your coworker's eyes as you reveal the special person's name.

What You'll Need

A piece of paper

A fine-tip red marker

A black permanent marker (like a Sharpie)

What You'll Do

1. Prepare for this trick by writing the numbers 1 to 5 down the left side of a piece of paper.

2. Now secretly touch the tip of the red pen with the tip of the black marker.

3. Ask your coworker to use the red pen to first write down his mentor's name, then the names of four people who were not as influential. He can write down any name next to any number.

4. When your coworker writes down the first name with the red pen, a dot of black will appear at the tip of the very first letter.

5. The black dot is your clue to the influential name they have selected, because this was the first name written. (You may want to experiment with the pen and marker beforehand, so that the black dot is noticeable only to you.)

6. Reveal the mentor's name: "I feel that the most influential person in your life is _____. Tell me a little more about him."

Now watch as your coworker's face fills with wonder!

(*Warning:* You are now one of the few people in on this magician's secret. *Please keep it a secret.* The fewer who know, the greater the effect.)

How to Get Someone to Believe Money Really Does Grow on Trees

No one these days will fall for the old banana-in-the-tailpipe trick. But almost everyone will buy the burned-up-dollar-bill-reappearing-inside-an-orange trick, especially if you pull it off in the company lounge. (*Warning:* The cries of disbelief will most likely rouse the boss's attention, so try to keep it down in there.)

What They See

You request a dollar bill from a colleague. You immediately sign the bill and have another colleague copy down the serial number. You fold the bill, place it into a small envelope, and set it on fire. You say, "Ashes to ashes, dust to dust, the dollar bill is no longer among us." But now the real magic begins. You ask your colleague to remove an orange from a nearby fruit bowl and ask him to peel it open. Lo and behold! The signed dollar bill with the same serial number is *inside the orange!*

What You'll Need

Two new dollar bills with consecutive serial numbers (obtain these
  from your neighborhood bank)

A small envelope (letter size or smaller)

A box of matches

A bowl of fruit

An orange with the stem still attached

A pencil

A confederate

What You'll Do

Some careful preparation is the key to success for this trick. Be sure you've put a box of matches in your pocket beforehand.

1. Obtain two new dollar bills from your bank. Request that the serial numbers on the bills be consecutive (i.e., the final digit should be one number apart; the rest of the numbers and letters should be exactly the same).

2. Erase the last number on two of the bills (the serial numbers appear on the right and left sides of the front of the bill), thereby creating duplicate bills.

3. Sign, fold, then roll one of the duplicate bills into the shape of a small tube.

4. Remove the small green stem from an orange.

5. Using a pen or pencil, poke a hole into the orange and push the bill into the center of the orange. (Fig. A) (Be careful not to poke the pencil all the way through to the other side of the rind!)

6. Glue the stem back in place, and put the orange on top of the fruit bowl.

Fig. A. Use a pencil or pen to poke a hole in the orange so you can push the bill into its center.

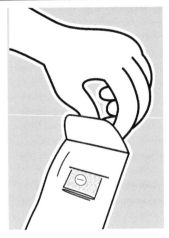

Fig. B. Once you've folded the bill into quarters, place it into the envelope so that the bill protrudes through the small slit.

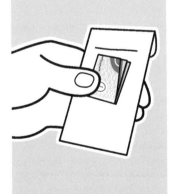

Fig. C. Secretly remove the protruding bill from the slit by holding the envelope in your hand with the slit concealed from your audience.

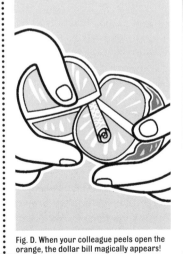

Fig. D. When your colleague peels open the orange, the dollar bill magically appears!

7. Cut a small slit into the back of the envelope. (The slit should be big enough for a bill folded in quarters to pass through.)

8. Arrange with another coworker to act as your confederate: hand him one of the duplicate bills you created.

9. Now you're ready for your audience. As above, ask your confederate for a dollar bill. (He'll hand you your gimmicked bill.)

10. Sign the bill, and ask a second colleague to write down the bill's serial number.

11. Fold the bill in quarters and place it in the envelope, making sure that the bill protrudes through the small slit you created. (Fig. B)

12. As you seal the envelope, secretly remove the protruding bill from the concealed slit. (To do this, hold the envelope so that the slit faces toward you, and away from your audience. [Fig. C] As you search for your matches with your other hand, remove the bill from the envelope and pocket it.)

13. Light a match to the envelope and let it burn completely.

14. As above, ask your second colleague to retrieve the top orange and peel it open. (Fig. D) Aside from his surprise at finding a dollar in an orange, your coworker will be completely amazed to find that the bill's serial number exactly matches the one he wrote down!

How to Make Paper Clips
Link Themselves

You've called your phone and no one's home, your Web connection is being monitored, and you already ate all of your trail mix . . . so how else can you look busy as you stare at that spreadsheet on your desk? Two words: paper clips. As long as you're having fun with office supplies, why not entertain the rest of the office?

What They See

You bind together eight small, unlinked paper clips with a rubber band. You wave them over a lit match and say some magic words. You have a coworker remove the rubber band, and—voilà!—now the clips are all linked together!

What You'll Need

16 identical small paper clips

Two identical plain rubber bands

A match

What You'll Do

1. This trick requires a small amount of preparation, out of sight of your audience. First, link together a string of eight paper clips and wrap a rubber band around them. (Fig. A)

Fig. A. Link the clips together and wrap a rubber band around them.

Fig. B. While you dig around in your pockets for a match, switch the bundle with the prepared bundle in your pocket.

Fig. C. Wave the switched bundle over the lit flame.

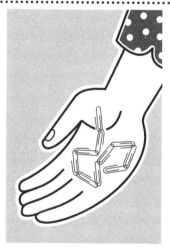

Fig. D. Have your coworker undo the rubber band—the unlinked clips have become linked!

2. Place this bundle in your coat or pants pocket.

3. Now you're ready for your audience. Gather around a group of your coworkers and show them a handful of eight unlinked paper clips.

4. Take your rubber band and wrap it around the clips. (This bundle now looks identical to the pre-prepared bundle you have in your pocket.)

5. Ask one of your colleagues to examine the clips and hand the bundle back to you.

6. Now ask if anyone has a match. Pretend to dig around in your own pocket for a match; meanwhile switch the one bundle for the prepared bundle in your pocket. (Fig. B) (This motion should appear quite natural so no one will suspect a switch was made.)

7. Once you pull the paper clips out of your pocket, pull a book of matches from the opposite pocket.

8. Light one of the matches.

9. Now wave the switched bundle over the lit flame and say the magic words: "Hocus, pocus, link the clips before us!" (Fig. C)

10. Have one of your coworkers undo the rubber band to show that the unlinked clips magically have become linked! (Fig. D)

How to Make a Banana Appear Out of Thin Air—and Make It Split

With a little preparation—and an early lunch break—you can be the hit of the company cafeteria. Who else do you know in your company who can make a banana appear out of nowhere and then chop it into three even pieces with his bare hand! Jackie Chan you ain't . . . but Harry Houdini, why not?

What They See

The first part of this trick is really very simple: Using your conjuring powers, you are able to make a banana appear out of thin air. Then, to the amazement of all who've gathered around, you karate-chop the banana into three perfectly sliced pieces!

What You'll Need

A banana

A straight pin or straightened paper clip

What You'll Do

1. First, a small amount of banana preparation is in order. Before you enter the lunchroom, get your hands on a banana and a straight pin or a straightened paper clip.

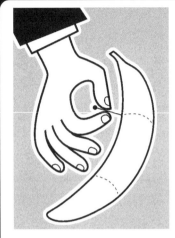

Fig. A. Insert the pin and move it back and forth so that you cut the banana without cutting the skin.

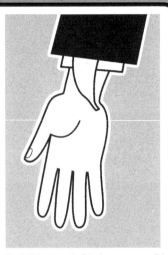

Fig. B. Hide as much of the banana as possible up your sleeve.

Fig. C. Quickly bring your hands together so that the banana flies to your fingertips.

Fig. D. Pretend to throw some karate chops at the banana.

2. You will now slice the banana without slicing through the skin, using the straight pin or straightened paperclip. Insert the pin a third of the way down the banana and move it back and forth so that you cut the banana inside but leave the skin uncut. (Fig. A)

3. Repeat this from the opposite end of the banana, so that the second cut is a third of the way down.

4. Now you're ready to enter the lunchroom. Hide the banana in your hand by slipping as much as possible up your sleeve. (Fig. B)

5. Beginning with your hands at your sides, quickly bring your hands together so that the banana flies to your fingertips. Since your audience does not know what you are about to do, the production of the banana will catch them off guard. (Fig. C)

6. Now that you have the banana, you're ready to perform some real magic. Ask one of your lunch mates which number he likes best, 2 or 3?

7. Have this person hold the banana in front of him as you go into your karate stance.

8. Now throw invisible karate chops at the banana. (Fig. D) If your colleague chooses 2, you will create 2 cuts. If he chooses 3, you will create 3 pieces. (Either way, you can't lose!)

9. Now have your coworker peel the banana to reveal how sharp your karate chops really are: You've split the banana into three pieces!

How to Spend Your Quarterly Earnings

You've just been promoted to head crony, and it's your turn to run the depart-
mental meeting. You have the floor for the first time. Your knees are knocking,
your forehead is glistening, as all wait with baited breath to hear about the company's quarterly earnings. Suddenly, you're simply unable to picture them all
naked, and you've forgotten all your jokes. . . . *How will you survive the meeting
without making a complete fool of yourself?* Time to try some quarterly magic!

What They See

You borrow a quarter (or other medium-size coin) from a colleague and have
her mark it with a felt-tip pen for future identification. You place the quarter
under a handkerchief. You have your colleague hold the quarter by its edge,
while it is under the handkerchief. But when you quickly snatch the handkerchief away, the quarter has vanished! Now you reach into your pocket and
pull out the marked quarter.

What You'll Need

A necktie or long scarf

A quarter (or any other medium-size coin)

A felt-tip pen

A handkerchief

Fig. A. Fasten the coin inside the tip of your necktie or scarf.

Fig. B. Using your handkerchief to conceal your move, lean forward and secretly bring up the quarter that is in the tip of your tie and position it beneath the handkerchief.

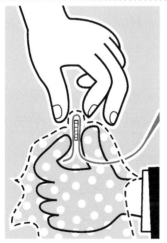

Fig. C. Ask your colleague to hold onto the edge of the coin, through the handkerchief.

Fig. D. Quickly snatch the handkerchief away so that the coin in your tie is simultaneously jerked from your colleague's hand. Voilà—the coin has vanished!

What You'll Do

You'll have to wear a necktie or scarf for this trick.

1. Before you enter the room, fasten a quarter inside the tip of your necktie or scarf. This can be done by slipping it into the hem of the tie or scarf (or by simply sewing the quarter into the hem). (Fig. A)

2. Now you're ready to take the floor. Ask a colleague for a quarter and have her mark it with a felt-tip pen.

3. Take your colleague's quarter and pretend to cover it with your handkerchief, placing it in the center. Instead, lean forward and secretly bring up the quarter that is in the tip of your tie or scarf and place it beneath the handkerchief while you retain your coworker's quarter in your hand. (Fig. B)

4. Have your coworker hold onto the edge of the cloth-covered quarter. (Fig. C)

5. Now quickly snatch the hankie away to show that the quarter has vanished. When you snatch the handkerchief away, the quarter your colleague is holding (the one in your tie/scarf) is jerked from her hand as you let the tie/scarf fall back into its natural position. (Fig. D)

6. Reach into your pocket and pretend to withdraw your coworker's original marked quarter (which you've been hiding in your hand all along).

A Little Add-on Trick

This one's sure to produce a few groans. When your coworker takes the coin from her pocket say, "I bet I can tell you the date." As she holds the coin tightly in her fist, you tell her the correct date—not the date on the quarter, of course, but the *current calendar date*!

How to Snake-Charm
a Pencil

Stand back as we attempt to capture and charm the most poisonous lead on your desk—the diamondback Number 2 pencil! (*Warning:* Never do this trick with a mechanical pencil. It's far too dangerous.)

What They See

You drop a pencil into an empty soda bottle, and you're ready to go. With a few little toots on your kazoo, the pencil magically begins to rise in the bottle. When the pencil is almost to the very top of the bottle, you snatch it and hand it to one of your coworkers. She can now examine all of the props—but she'll find nothing but an ordinary soda bottle and pencil!

What You'll Need

An empty soda bottle

A kazoo

A pencil

Clear sewing thread (purchased at your local fabric store) about
18 inches long

A razor blade

Fig. A. Slip one end of the sewing thread into the slit you've cut in the eraser.

Fig. B. Attach the other end of the thread to a button on your shirt.

Fig. C. As you play your kazoo, wave your free hand in front of the bottle, so that the thread is forced against your wrist and the pencil begins to rise.

Fig. D. When the pencil reaches the top of the bottle, drop the kazoo and snatch the pencil so that the thread is pulled free.

What You'll Do

1. Some preparation is in order here. Before you perform this trick, use a razor blade to make a small slice in the eraser of the pencil.

2. Slip one end of the sewing thread into the slit. (Fig. A)

3. Attach the other end of the thread to a button on your shirt. (Simply twist the thread around the button a few times.) (Fig. B)

4. Now you're ready for your audience. Drop the pencil into the bottle, eraser-side down.

5. As you blow into your kazoo, gracefully wave your free hand in front of the bottle. As you are doing this, the thread will be forced against your wrist and the pencil will begin to rise from the bottle. (Fig. C)

6. When the pencil reaches the top of the bottle, snatch the pencil from the bottle. (Fig. D) As you do this, the thread will be pulled from the eraser, so your audience can inspect every part of the trick without catching on.

Everyone who sees this tricked is bound to be charmed.

How to Create a
Potato Chip Surprise

Does your desk seem to be the company snacking center? Do your co-workers wait until you return from the vending machine to come up, ask you a question, and dip into your potato chips? If you're too kind to yell, or too timid to ask, use this potato chip surprise to get them to stop eating your food!

What They See

You open a small bag of potato chips. Any flavor will do. You ask your coworker if he knows what's in a potato chip these days: "Have you ever read some of the ingredients in your favorite foods? Most times you need a Ph.D. just to pronounce the words on the package. What about the things that *aren't* listed on the package?"

As you read the ingredients from the bag, to his surprise you pull a ruler out of the bag!

What You'll Need

A bag of potato chips

A ruler or table utensil

A long-sleeved shirt or jacket

A sharp knife or razor blade

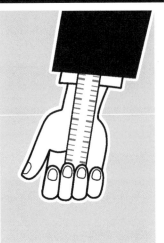

Fig. A. Drop your hand down, allowing a small section of the ruler to fall into your palm.

Fig. B. Place the bag into the palm that's holding the ruler and dump out the chips.

Fig. C. Reach into the bag of chips, get hold of the ruler through the slit, and pull it into the bag.

Fig. D. Pull the ruler from the bag—to the amazement of your audience!

What You'll Do

1. To prepare for this trick you must first slip a ruler up your sleeve.

2. Now make a 1-inch slit with a sharp knife or razor blade in the lower back panel of your chip bag. If you can manage to do this before your audience arrives on the scene, do so; otherwise, do this under the desk as you chat. (You can use the patter printed above under "What They See.")

3. Drop your hand down, allowing a small section of the ruler to fall into your palm. (Fig. A)

4. Now place the bag into the palm that's holding the ruler, tear open the bag, and dump the chips onto your desk. (Fig. B)

5. With your opposite hand, reach into the bag and pull the ruler through the slit in the back of the bag. (Fig. C) Presto—the perfect potato chip surprise! (Fig. D)

How to Make a Calculator Predict the Future

Picture yourself at your monthly budget meeting. The numbers are not quite adding up, and the tension in the room is mounting. Where will that $5,000 come from to pay for the new workout room? Where will you get that extra $3,700 to pay for the bathroom-mounted video system? Why not loosen up the proceedings with a nifty trick of calculated telepathy? If nothing else, it will get everyone's attention away from the fact that your department was over budget by 10 percent last quarter.

What They See

You have three colleagues each think of a three-digit number, with each of the digits being different. (For example: 523.) Meanwhile, you write down a predicted number and seal it in an envelope. Using a calculator, you add up their numbers. The total matches your sealed prediction, which has been resting on the table the whole time, untouched until the moment of revelation.

What You'll Need

Any ordinary calculator (as long as it has a memory button)

An envelope

A slip of paper

What You'll Do

1. Ask your colleagues to think of their three-digit numbers.

2. Meanwhile, prepare your prediction in a sealed envelope and place it on the table. When you have three people participating, a good number to "predict" would be 1,492. This will be in the ballpark of the actual sum of their three numbers, and will seem plausible to the participants.

3. As you turn on the calculator, secretly punch this same number on the keypad and press the M+ (Memory Save) key. This will save your "predicted" number.

4. Have each participant enter his three-digit number as you hand the calculator to each of them in turn: After the first and second partici- pants enter their numbers, hit the "+" key, then pass the calculator to the last participant. (Make sure this person is not a mathematical genius, because he'd be the only one in the room with a clue as to what has transpired.)

5. When "totaling" the three numbers, **do not hit the "Total" key**— make sure you hit the MR (Memory Recall) button instead.

6. Now have one of your colleagues open the sealed envelope.

Presto—your prediction has come true!

How to Perform Telepathy with the Company Directory

Does it seem like everyone in your office is getting a promotion except for you? Does it seem like the boss doesn't even know your name? Does it seem like you can miss a day of work and no one notices? (If you answered yes to any of these questions, **do not** read on: you've achieved the good life—take the day off and go fishing!) If any of this is starting to get to you, try this dumbfounding company directory telepathy trick—it will get you noticed in no time. Pull this one off and everyone will be impressed with your powers of perception.

What They See

You hand a sealed envelope to your boss for safekeeping. You ask that one of your coworkers step forward, and you hand the company directory to her. You ask her to flip the directory open to any page, close her eyes, and put her finger on a random name. She opens her eyes and reads the name out loud. When the envelope is opened, a slip of paper inside reveals that you wrote down the very same name!

What You'll Need

A slip of paper

A pen

An envelope

Your company directory

A confederate

What You'll Do

1. Before your performance you must acquire a secret helper. This confederate coworker will naturally step forward as your volunteer as you begin the trick. She will follow your simple directions (see steps 4–6, below), but will say the name "Harry Keller" (see note, below) no matter which name her finger falls on.

2. Begin the trick by writing "Harry Keller" on a slip of paper and sealing the slip in an envelope. Have your boss place the envelope in the center of the conference table.

3. Ask for a "volunteer." (Your confederate, of course, is the chosen one.)

4. Ask your coworker to flip open the directory to any page.

5. As she holds the book in one hand, ask her to close her eyes and, with her other hand, place her finger down either the right or left page.

6. Ask her to reveal the name her finger landed on—with the added instruction that if her finger has landed on a phone number, she should go to the corresponding name.

7. Ask your boss to open the envelope and read your prediction out loud. Unbelievable, but true—you predicted the very same name! Now take a bow to the thunderous applause of your appreciative audience!

Tip: Get as elaborate as you like when writing your prediction. For example:

I, [your name here], on this day of [fill in the date], predict that the name freely selected from the phone book will be Harry Keller.

You can even have this document notarized by another coworker just to make it an even more believable effect.

Note: "Harry Keller" is used here as an example only. It is very important that the name you choose to use is in fact in the directory. The name you use should start with the letter "K" because the Ks are found in the center of the book. The instructions that you give the spectator are also very important—they heighten the level of misdirection, and no one will catch on that your volunteer is actually a confederate. (Most observers assume that the trick must be in the directory or the procedure itself.)

How to Make Time Fly

Tick-tock, tick-tock. No matter how hard you try, that clock just won't move any faster. Five o'clock seems as far away now as it was two hours ago. How many more times can you pick up a pile of papers from your desk, walk them to your coworker's, and then return ten minutes later to pick them up—all in an attempt to appease the manager who's carefully monitoring your movements from his corner office? Next time you venture to your coworker's desk, give this trick a try—at least you'll kill a few minutes.

What They See

Gathering several coworkers around you, you ask for someone to volunteer their watch, and you direct them to spin the stem several times to arrive at a random time of day. You write down a few numbers on a piece of paper, then seal your slip in an envelope. Someone opens up your sealed envelope, revealing that the numbers you wrote indicate the same time!

What You'll Need

An analog watch that also shows the date

An envelope

A slip of paper

A pencil

What You'll Do

1. Ask one of your coworkers for an analog watch that displays both time and date.

2. Pull out the stem and demonstrate that the hands spin freely. (Fig. A)

3. Remembering the time at which you stopped, turn the watch face-down and secretly push the stem in one notch—which is the date position.

4. Ask for a volunteer to come up and spin the stem as often as he wishes, backward or forward, keeping the watch face down.

5. As your volunteer is freely spinning the stem, write down your prediction and seal it in the envelope. (Fig. B) Be sure to leave the envelope in view of your audience.

6. When your volunteer has finished spinning the stem, ask him to push it in, locking the hands in place. Don't worry—he's only changing the date, even though he assumes he's moving the hands. (Fig. C)

7. Next, have him turn the watch over and read the time.

8. Now have him open your prediction, which has been sitting in front of the group the whole time. Your prediction will be accurate within minutes of the selected time. (Fig. D)

Note: You *could* have predicted the time to the precise second, but being a few minutes off makes this effect more believable.

Fig. A. Pull out the stem and demonstrate that the hands spin freely.

Fig. B. While your volunteer freely spins the stem, write down your prediction and seal it in an envelope.

Fig. C. Ask your volunteer to push the stem in, locking the hands in place.

Fig. D. Have your volunteer open your prediction—which will be accurate within minutes of the selected time!

How to Make Jelly Bean Magic
with a Breath Mints Box

Simple chronic halitosis: a complicated term, a common problem. Every
office has at least one person who has the malady but refuses to admit
it. Next time ol' Hal E. Tosis comes visiting *your* desk, give this trick a try.
Who could resist the lure of those tasty jelly beans? If nothing else, you'll at
least be covering up that unpleasant odor for a minute or two, and entertaining your coworkers while you're at it.

What They See

You show your coworkers a breath mints box that you've filled with six
different-colored jelly beans. You display a sample of each flavor in front of
one of your colleagues. You ask him to give you a number between 1 and 6,
and you place the corresponding jelly bean in his hand. You ask, "Wouldn't
it be wonderful if you could get a box of jelly beans filled with the flavor of
your choice?" When you spill the contents of the tin into his hand, they're all
his favorite bean!

What You'll Need

An empty tin of breath mints with a simple hinged lid

Some glue

Enough jelly beans to fill the box, in six different colors

What You'll Do

This trick will require some bean preparation time.

1. Take one bean of each color and set them aside.

2. Prepare your tin by gluing down all of the beans, except those that are orange-colored (or any other single color of your choosing). (Fig. A) Your orange-colored beans are left loose in the tin. (Fig. B)

3. Now you're ready for your audience. Take the beans from step 1 and line them up in a row in front of your coworker. Make sure that the orange bean is in the third position from the left.

4. Ask your coworker to name a number between 1 and 6. No matter what number your coworker gives you, you are going to "force" the third bean:

   If they pick 1, spell "o-n-e" from left to right.

   If they pick 2, spell "t-w-o" from left to right.

   If they pick 3, count "1-2-3" from left to right.

   If they pick 4, count "1-2-3-4" from right to left.

   If they pick 5, spell "f-i-v-e" from right to left.

   If they pick 6, spell "s-i-x" from left to right.

5. Now, place the "chosen" orange bean from the third position into his hand. (Fig. C)

6. Empty the contents of the tin. A cascade of his favorite orange jelly-beans falls into his hand!

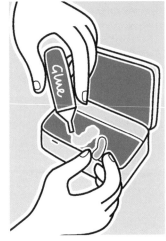

Fig. A. Glue down all of the beans, except those that are, for example, orange-colored.

Fig. B. The orange-colored beans are left loose in the box.

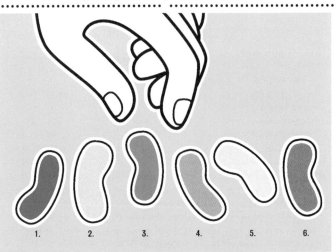

1.   2.   3.   4.   5.   6.

Fig. C. Place the bean from the third position into your coworker's hand.

Note: Needless to say, this is not a trick that can be immediately repeated! Once you've gimmicked the box for this performance, you're tied in to "forcing" the bean you've glued down in advance. (If your coworkers ask to see the trick again, simply explain that your magical powers have been sapped for the day.)

Chapter 3

MAGIC ON THE GO

These days, everyone from workaday commuters to soccer moms rack up hundreds of miles every week. By plane, by train, by automobile—we're constantly on the go. The good news: everyday magic is completely portable, easily packable, and always ready to roll. With a little bit of preparation and just the right amount of showmanship, you can pull a magic trick out of your hat, your suitcase, your knapsack—whenever and wherever.

Is that meter maid about to write you a ticket? Try magically talking your way out of it by turning a dollar bill into a coin! Are you stuck on the tracks again? Try putting smiles on the faces of your fellow commuters with ingenious newspaper magic! Are your onboard companions getting cranky? Try entertaining them by catching a ghost in an airsickness bag!

You get the idea—no matter where you are, no matter where you're going, you can use your magical powers to make the most of your time on the go!

How to Magically Feed a Parking Meter

Why is it that when you've raced to your car, ready to put more money in the meter, the parking cops just pretend not to see you? As soon as that pen hits the pad, they simply act like you're not there, and nothing will get in the way of their writing up a ticket. The next time this happens to you, why not try a little magic to get their attention? There's no better way to avoid a ticket, and you may even make a new friend to boot!

What You'll Need

A dollar bill

A coin

What They See

You remove a dollar from your pocket, showing the front and the back. You then proceed to fold the dollar into fourths, lengthwise. *Kerplop*—out drops a coin! You swiftly place the coin in the meter and tell the cop to have a nice day.

What You'll Do

1. Remove a dollar bill from your pocket, along with a coin.

2. Hold the dollar with both hands (Fig. A) and conceal the coin under

Fig. A. Hold the bill with both hands so that the front of the bill faces the cop.

Fig. B. Hide the coin under your right thumb, so that it's concealed behind the bill.

Fig. C. Wrap the bill around the coin in fourths, holding the coin with your right thumb and index finger.

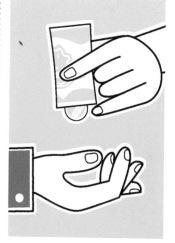

Fig. D. Let the coin drop into the cop's hand!

your right thumb (with the front of the dollar facing the cop). (Fig. B)

3. Release the bill with your left hand and carefully turn the dollar around to expose the back of the dollar to the cop, with the coin now concealed by your left-hand fingertips.

4. Now turn the dollar back to the starting position, retaining the coin once again under the right thumb. You have now clearly shown the front and back of the dollar.

5. Wrap the dollar around the coin in fourths, holding the coin in place with your right thumb and index fingers. (Fig. C) The dollar will naturally fold into four equal pieces.

6. Ask the cop to hold out his hand.

7. Let the coin drop into the cop's hand. (Fig. D)

8. While the cop shakes his head in amazement, pluck the coin from his hand and feed your meter.

If That Fails to Do the Trick

If the coin trick fails to charm, you may need to resort plan B: **How to Make Yourself Cry.** Few traffic cops are immune to the sight of a grown man or woman in tears over a parking ticket.

What They See

Tears flowing from your eyes

What You'll Need

A small piece of tissue (about 2 inches square)

A water bottle

What You'll Do

1. Before approaching the car, dip a 2-inch square piece of napkin or tissue into your water bottle.

2. Roll the damp tissue into a small ball, retaining some liquid in it.

3. Keep this ball of tears in a nearby pocket. When you drop the coin into the cop's hand, secretly pick up the ball of tears.

4. Pick up the coin from the cop's hand and conceal the tear ball behind it with your thumb.

5. Merely squeeze the tissue and allow the tears to flow.

How to Bend a Spoon with Your Psychokinetic Powers

Just about everyone over the age of seven knows how to hang a spoon off their face. Why, we once observed the restaurant record of *seven* spoons—one on the nose, one on each cheek, one on the chin, one on each ear, and one on top of the head! It was amazing. This next trick is even more amazing, and will set you a cut above the ordinary seven-year-old. Try it the next time you're traveling by train and want to create a little diversion in the dining car—just be sure to ask for a metal spoon, not the plastic kind.

What They See

You tell your audience that you have psychokinetic powers. You pick up a spoon by the handle and hold it so that the very tip is exposed above your index finger. You proceed to bend the spoon in half with your mind's powers alone! Next, you cover it with a handkerchief or napkin. Just a little concentration and a magical wave of your hand and—Shazam! You remove the handkerchief from the spoon, and it has been restored to its original condition!

What You'll Need

A spoon

A small silver coin

A napkin (cloth or paper) or handkerchief

Fig. A. Secretly place the coin at the tip of the spoon handle so that it mimics the end of the spoon.

Fig. B. Cover the spoon handle with both hands so that only the very tip and the end of the spoon are exposed.

Fig. C. (single-hand view): As seen here, one of your clasped hands will hold both the coin and the bottom of the spoon.

Fig. D. Bring the coin forward while you slide the spoon so that it lays flat on the table. From your audience's perspective, the spoon appears to bend!

What You'll Do

It's best to be sitting at a table when you perform this trick.

1. Before your audience arrives on the scene, palm the small coin so that it's hidden from view.

2. Secretly place the coin at the tip of the spoon handle so that it looks like the end of the spoon. (Fig. A)

3. Holding the spoon vertically, cover the spoon handle with both hands, allowing only the top (containing the coin) and bottom ends of the spoon to be exposed. (Fig. B)

4. Bring the coin forward while you slide the spoon so that it lays flat on the table. (Figs. C–D) This will give the illusion that the spoon is being bent.

5. Cover the spoon with a handkerchief or napkin and ditch the coin in your lap.

6. After a bit of magical hand waving and intense concentration, you now have the spectator remove the handkerchief. Of course it will be completely restored!

How to Magically Force a Bottle Cap Through a Bottle

Have you always wanted to be one of those macho guys who can smash a beer can into his head? Well, here's your chance to do a comparable trick—without any risk of brain damage!—the next time you're out for a bike ride with your pals.

What They See

You pull out an ordinary plastic bottle of spring water (or soda). You announce to your friends that you can force the plastic bottle top into the bottle with your sheer brute strength. You screw off the bottle cap, and smash it into the bottle. Presto! The cap has penetrated into the bottle.

What You'll Need

An empty plastic soda or water bottle, with its original cap

A single-edge razor blade or sharp pocketknife

Clear, fast-drying glue

What You'll Do

1. Before you go out on your ride, locate the seam on the bottle's label and carefully peel it back a half-inch.

2. Using a single-edged razor blade, cut a vertical slit into the plastic

bottle underneath the portion of the label you've just lifted. The vertical slit should be just a tad shorter than the width of the label and large enough so that the cap can be inserted inside it.

3. Work the cap into the slit. (The plastic will give some resistance.)

4. Carefully return the label flap to its original position. There should be enough glue on the label to paste the flap down again. If there is no glue on the label, use a fast-drying, clear glue to secure it.

5. You're now ready for your audience. Hold the bottom of the bottle in your left hand, so that the cap inside the bottle is entirely concealed from your audience's view. Your fingers should curve around the front of the bottle so that there's no way anyone can see the cap. (Try practicing this in a mirror to get just the right effect.)

6. Hold the top of the bottle with your right hand so that no one can see that the bottle has no cap.

7. Now, as you pretend to unscrew the cap with your right hand, tell your friends that you can make the cap penetrate to the bottom of the bottle.

8. Mime the motion of removing the cap, and then pretend that you are holding it in your right fist.

9. Now smash the bottom of the bottle down into your left palm as you quickly open your right fist. It looks like your brute force has forced the cap into the bottle!

10. Hand the bottle around for inspection. The slit will not be noticed—it's hidden by the joining seam on the label.

How to Entertain a Group of Angry Commuters with a Newspaper

The 7:59 train is stuck on the tracks. Trains all around are whizzing by. Then comes the dreaded announcement: due to equipment failure, your train won't be going anywhere for at least an hour. As the cell phones are whipped out and the grumbling reaches a fever-pitch, you step to the front of the car and wow your fellow commuters with a trick so amazing they'd spend the rest of the day waiting on the train with you if they could.

What They See

You fold in half a 2-foot strip of newspaper about 2 inches wide. With your handy Swiss army knife, you cut an inch from the top, and the piece falls to the floor. It now appears that you have two pieces of newspaper. When you open the strip in your hands, however, you reveal that the newspaper is still in one piece!

What You'll Need

A strip of newspaper about 2 inches wide and 2 feet long

Rubber cement

Baby powder

Scissors or a Swiss army knife

Fig. A. After you have coated one side of the newspaper strip with rubber cement and let it dry, sprinkle it with baby powder and shake off the excess.

Fig. B. Fold the strip in half so that the rubber cement is on the inside and the fold is at the top.

Fig. C. Cut off the top inch of the paper.

Fig. D. Carefully unfold the strip to show that the paper is still in one piece!

What You'll Do

This trick requires that you prepare the gimmicked newspaper beforehand. The good news is, the prepped newspaper can be carried around for a full week before you actually do the trick.

1. Cut a piece of newspaper about 2 inches wide by about 2 feet long.

2. Coat one side of the paper with rubber cement and let it dry.

3. After it has dried, sprinkle it with some baby powder and shake off the excess. (Fig. A)

4. Now you're ready to face your audience. Fold the strip in half so that the rubber cement is on the inside and the fold is at the top. (Fig. B)

5. Cut off the top inch as described in "What They See." (Fig. C)

6. Now carefully unfold the strip to show that the paper is still intact. (Fig. D) The rubber cement will hold the cut edges together quite nicely!

How to Catch a Ghost
in an Airsickness Bag

You're on the plane, your bag is stowed, your seatback is up, and your seatbelt is on. Trouble is, you've just been informed that, due to heavy traffic, your plane will not be taking off for at least an hour. Your fellow passengers could sure use some entertainment. With a little help from this amazing ghost-in-an-airsickness-bag trick, you're sure to delight even the crankiest of your seatmates.

What They See

You show your fellow passengers the front and back of a handkerchief. You lay the handkerchief flat on your tray table and fold all the corners into the center. You swipe at the air to catch a "ghost" and place it into the center of the hankie. Your seatmates will see a shape materialize under the handkerchief. Use a pen to tap on the shape. It's definitely there!

What You'll Need

A white handkerchief

An old credit card that you're about to discard

A pen

A white stick-on label

An airsickness bag

Fig. A. Fold all four corners into the center of the handkerchief. The first corner you fold in should contain the plastic piece.

Fig. B. Pinching the first corner with your fingers, flip the handkerchief over, pretending to catch your "ghost" in the air.

Fig. C. Hold the airsickness bag so that all of your fingers are in the bag, but your thumb remains outside.

Fig. D. With the hand that's holding the bag, snap your fingers. That's the sound of the ghost falling into the bag!

What You'll Do

This trick will require a bit of advance preparation before you board the plane.

1. Cut a piece from the credit card (approximately ¼ inch by 2½ inches) and push it into the hem of the handkerchief. If your handkerchief has no hem, you can glue or stitch the piece of credit card in place. To better conceal the piece of credit card, cover it with a white stick-on label.

2. Now you're ready for your audience. Show the handkerchief front and back.

3. Lay the handkerchief flat on your tray table.

4. Fold all four corners into the center of the handkerchief, making sure that the first corner you fold in contains the piece of credit card. (Fig. A)

5. Pinching the first corner with your fingers, flip the hankie over and pretend to catch your ghost from the air. As you do this, stand the credit card on end. (Fig. B)

6. Use the pen to tap on the top of the plastic. Your seatmates can hear you tapping on the "ghost" and are *sure* there's something there!

7. Take the handkerchief and give it a flick, showing that there's nothing at all in the handkerchief.

8. Now take hold of your airsickness bag with one hand. Hold it so that all of your fingers are in the bag and your thumb is outside the bag. (Fig. C)

9. Pretend to throw the ghost up into the air.

10. As your friendly ghost falls, pretend to catch him in the bag.

11. Now snap your fingers with the hand that is holding the bag so that everyone can hear the ghost fall into the bag! (Fig. D)

How to Use House Keys to Predict the Future

Con men have been known to use a particularly slick method of guaranteeing a winner. It's called touting, and it assures that whoever they want to win, will win. Now, thanks to *Amazing Irv's Handbook of Everyday Magic*, you too can be a con man . . . er, use the con man's method to make a little magic. Pull this one on your friend who's running the three-card monty on the street corner. You might just be able to win some of your money back.

What They See

You remove three keys from your key chain, each one a different color. Removing a pen from your pocket, you ask your friend to select one of the colored keys by touching it with the pen. You now reveal to your friend that you knew precisely which key he'd pick, and you have the physical evidence to prove it.

What You'll Need

Three keys, each with a different color head (purchased at your local
  hardware store)

A pen with a clear barrel

A slip of paper

A sticker

A key case

What You'll Do

Are you ready to learn how to predict the future? It's easier than you can imagine. Before you even begin the trick, you will have made three separate predictions. Depending on the key your friend touches with the pen, you will present the corresponding prediction.

1. Place a piece of paper in the barrel of the pen that says, "You have picked red." If your friend picks the red key, show him the message in the pen's barrel.

2. In your key case, place a piece of paper that says, "You have picked green." If your friend picks the green key, show him the message in your key case.

3. On the back of the yellow-headed key, place a small sticker that says, "You have picked yellow." If your friend picks the yellow key, reveal the message on the back of the key.

No matter which key he picks, you will have predicted his choice exactly!

Note: Keep in mind that you can adapt this trick by using keys that vary in color, shape, and size. Your predictions must be adapted accordingly.

How to Be
a Cellular Psychic

Oh, those long family road trips sure are fun for everyone! Who would want to pass up the opportunity to rub legs with an obnoxious sibling in the back seat? Or sing show tunes in rounds from coast to coast? All right, so it gets a little old . . . but here's a little magic for those of you who want to break up the monotony at least for a few minutes. (*Warning:* This trick involves cell phones. If you are the designated driver and the designated magician, please check with your local legislature—or the legislature of the town you're driving through—to confirm whether or not cell phones and driving mix.)

What They See

You ask your captive audience for a volunteer. You tell this volunteer that you're about to prove that you have a special friend with amazing psychic abilities. You dial your friend's number on your cell phone, hand the phone to your volunteer, and tell him to ask for the Great Swami. You proceed to pick up various objects and hold them in your hand. Your volunteer asks the Swami what you're holding, and each time he asks, the Swami has the correct answer!

What You'll Need

A cell phone

A pair of sunglasses, a wristwatch, and any other small objects

A trusted friend

What You'll Do

The simplicity of this effect is its beauty.

1. You have prearranged with a friend that whenever she is called and the person asks for the Great Swami, she is ready with a prearranged list of items. A sample of these items could be: a pair of glasses, a wristwatch, a wallet, a pen, a left elbow—the list is limited only by your imagination.

2. Dial your friend's number then hand the phone to your volunteer, who will ask to speak to the Great Swami.

3. Remove your glasses and have your volunteer ask the Swami what is being held. She will instantly respond, "A pair of glasses."

4. Next, hold your watch in your fingertips and the Swami will announce that a watch is now being held. Whatever item you hold in your hand, the Swami will reveal it accurately.

The more your Swami hams it up, the better the effect!

How to Read Someone's Mind

Are you one of those people who likes to strike up conversations with complete strangers who just happen to have the good luck to be seated next to you on an airplane? Next time you're packing your carry-on bag, remember to bring along a deck of playing cards. After they see this fascinating trick of telepathy, there's no way they'll be able to concentrate on the in-flight movie!

What They See

To break the ice, you start off with a little patter: "A deck of cards is more than meets the eye. It contains 52 images—the same number of weeks in a year. There are four different suits—the same number of seasons in a year. There are 13 different values, ace through king—the same number of signs in the lunar calendar. And if you add up all the pips contained in a deck, you get 365 of them." Then you ask your travel companion to shuffle the deck. When she's satisfied that the deck is thoroughly mixed, you ask her to remember the bottom card and place the deck back into the box. There is no way you can possibly know her card, but you look into her eyes, and probe her mind. In seconds flat, you announce the card she chose.

Fig. A. Cut a small square hole in the bottom-right corner of the card box.

Fig. B. Hold your thumb over the hole while your friend returns the cards to the box.

Fig. C. As you place the box down on a table, move your thumb so that you can take a quick peek at the exposed card.

Fig. D. The pip will be visible through the cut in the box.

What You'll Need

A deck of cards

A razor blade

What You'll Do

1. Only one step of preparation is necessary, and you must do this before you leave your house: Using a razor blade, on the back of the box, cut a small square hole in the bottom-right corner. (Fig. A) This hole should be just large enough to get a glimpse at the pip of the bottom card.

2. Once on-board, try to remain natural as you remove the cards from the box; now ask your seatmate to shuffle the deck and remember the bottom card.

3. With your head turned so that you can't peek, hold the box so that she can return the deck to the box, bottom-card up. Be sure that your thumb conceals the hole as she places the cards back into the box. (Fig. B)

4. As you place the box down, casually move your thumb and take a peek. (Figs. C–D)

5. Now pretend to probe her mind, then slowly reveal her card. Example: "I see a black card—you're thinking of a club . . . I can't explain this but I am feeling the Queen of Clubs."

Act surprised when she confirms that you're right!

How to Make Magic
with a Paper Cup

That four-year old in the bus seat in front of you is so cute—or at least
she was an hour ago when she first started playing peek-a-boo with you.
You meant well when you started the game—you just didn't think it would
go on this long. Well, now you can bring those innocent games to a close,
as long as you've got a spare Dixie cup, a thumb, and a piece of string. (A
five-year-old with 20 years of experience can do this trick.)

What They See

You tie a loose knot at the end of a piece of rope or string. You lower the
knotted end into a paper cup, and when you pull the rope out of the cup,
the knot is gone!

What You'll Need

A large paper cup

A piece of rope or string about 12 inches long

What You'll Do

1. Before performing the trick, and out of sight of your audience, cut or
   punch a hole in the back side of your paper cup, about halfway down.
   The hole should be large enough to insert your thumb into. (Fig. A) Be

Fig. A. Cut or punch a hole in the back of a paper cup.

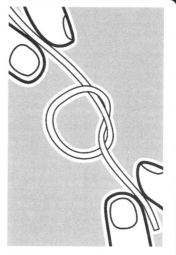

Fig. B. Tie a loose knot in the string.

Fig. C. Pick up the gimmicked cup and secretly slip your thumb into the hole.

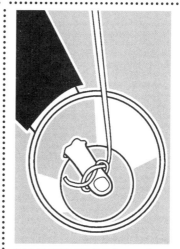

Fig. D. Lower the string into the cup, slip your thumb into the knot, and work it loose.

sure to keep the hole facing toward you, and away from your audience.

2. Now, tie a loose knot in the string or rope as your audience watches. (Fig. B)

3. Pick up the gimmicked cup and secretly insert your thumb into the hole. (Fig. C)

4. Lower the string into the cup, allowing your thumb to slip the knot. (Fig. D)

5. Now just pull the string out of the cup and—voilà! The knot is no more!

How to Make an Elephant Appear on a Moving Train

So you and your friends are returning home after a long weekend of party-ing. None of you has fully recovered enough to make the long train ride home enjoyable. In fact, it's downright miserable, and the aspirin you took last night didn't even touch the thumping in your head. Here's a little magic to take advantage of your friends' vulnerable state and shake the cobwebs out of your own head at the same time.

What They See

You tell your fellow passengers to close their eyes, because when they open them, they'll see that you've magically produced . . . *an elephant*. (Your excitement and enthusiasm are what sell this illusion.) When they do open their eyes, all they see is that you're holding a piece of paper with the word *elephant* spelled out on it. But after the smiles and boos, you roll the paper into a tube. When you tip the tube, out comes a handful of peanuts—clear evidence that the elephant *was* there but didn't finish his lunch.

What You'll Need

An 8$\frac{1}{2}$ x 11 inch piece of paper

A pen

Fig. A. Write the word *elephant* on a sheet of paper.

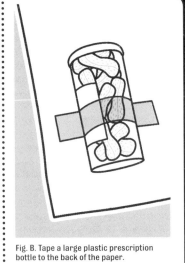

Fig. B. Tape a large plastic prescription bottle to the back of the paper.

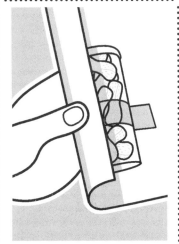

Fig. C. Roll the paper around the bottle, creating a paper tube.

Fig. D. Tip out the tube to produce the peanuts.

Adhesive tape

A handful of peanuts

A large prescription bottle

What You'll Do

1. This will require a small amount of preparation. Simply write the word *elephant* on your sheet of paper. (Fig. A)

2. On the back of the paper, tape a large plastic prescription bottle to the lower left edge. (Fig. B)

3. Fill the bottle with peanuts.

4. Now you're ready to perform. As above, ask your companions to close their eyes.

5. Bring out your gimmicked paper, and hold it so that they can read the word *elephant* but the bottle remains concealed from their view, behind the paper. (Be sure not to hold the paper so it's backlit, but do position your fingers on the paper so that they cover up the bottle's shadow.)

6. Now, roll the paper around the bottle, creating a paper tube. (Fig. C)

7. Tip the tube to produce the peanuts. (Fig. D)

Chapter 4

MAGIC ON THE TOWN

How many times has this happened to you:

You're out on the town with a date and neither one of you can think of anything to say.

You go to a club, only to see your date flirt with everyone but you.

You're walking your date home, when a mugger steps out of the shadows and demands all of your money.

You walk into the local diner to call your mother and ask her to come and pick you up; just before your date storms out, you explain that you really don't think 35 is too old to be living at home.

Okay, so maybe you'll be lucky enough never to find yourself in any of these unfortunate situations. But with the following sure-fire tricks for Magic on the Town, you'll never have to worry—you'll be prepared for all of these scenarios and more.

By following the simple instructions in the tricks that follow, you'll learn how to keep the romance alive at dinner by making magic with your sugar. You'll discover how to be the life of the party as you make your friend's drink vanish—into your coat pocket! And you'll learn that even muggers can get a kick out of watching you poke their knife blades through a five-dollar bill without making a hole.

In no time flat, you'll be making every night on the town a night to remember!

How to Use Coffee Shop X-Ray Vision

As if anybody ever needed help killing time at a coffee shop! Well, sometimes you just run out of papers to read, you're on your fifth latte, and there's—gasp!—a lull in the conversation. Everybody knows that a lull means . . . more coffee is required. Here's some sure-fire magic to help you decide who's going to buy the next round.

What They See

You present one of your friends with four coins of different sizes. You turn your back and ask him to select a coin. You have a second friend place a coffee cup over the coin and remove the remaining coins from view. Once they're done, you turn to face them and correctly reveal which coin has been covered.

What You'll Need

Four coins of different sizes

A coffee cup with a handle

A confederate

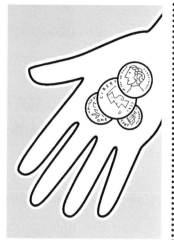

Fig. A. Present the four coins and place them on the table.

Fig. B. Ask one of your friends to choose a coin while your back is turned.

Fig. C. Your confederate will place the cup over the chosen coin and remove the others from view.

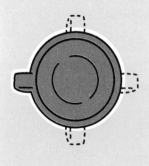

Fig. D. Your confederate will place the handle in the 12, 3, 6, or 9 o'clock position, depending on which coin was chosen.

What You'll Do

This trick requires the assistance of a trusted friend who will act as your confederate. Before you begin the trick, you and your confederate must review the signals in step 3, below.

1. As above, present the four coins and place them on the table. (Fig. A)

2. Turn your back and ask one of your friends to choose a coin. (Fig. B)

3. Ask your confederate to set the cup over the coin and remove the remaining coins from view. (Fig. C) When she places the cup over the coin, she'll place the handle in one of the following positions (Fig. D):

>   12 o'clock = Coin 1
>
>   3 o'clock = Coin 2
>
>   6 o'clock = Coin 3
>
>   9 o'clock = Coin 4

4. As you turn around to face your friend, you'll need only a quick glance to reveal which coin is under the cup!

Note: If your helper wants to let you know that your friend has done something tricky (he may not have put a coin under the cup at all or maybe he added another coin, like a half-dollar), she'll put the cup handle in any direction other than the ones above. In this event, you can say, "I think there's a problem here. I'm sensing that either there is no coin under the cup or a new coin has been added."

How to Make a Saltshaker Glow Like a Light Saber

Need to find a way to get the best seats for the latest *Star Wars* flick? All you have to do is show off your powers of the Force! Here's a surefire trick that will get you into the prime spot in no time—you simply have to wager some well-connected friends that you can make an ordinary saltshaker glow like a light saber! The winner gets first dibs on picking seats.

Tip: This trick works best when performed on people dressed as Yodas, Skywalkers, and Wookies. Do not perform this trick on people dressed as Darth Vaders or Storm Troopers.

What They See

You pick up what appears to be an ordinary saltshaker. In the blink of an eye, the salt crystals begin to glow.

What You'll Need

- A small, squeeze-activated flashlight (usually found on key chains you can buy at your local hardware store)
- A clear glass or plastic saltshaker

Fig. A. Pick up the saltshaker with your right hand and set it in your fisted left hand.

Fig. B. Give the saltshaker a magic tap while you squeeze the small flashlight with your opposite hand.

Fig. C. Presto!—the salt crystals will begin to glow!

Fig. D. Put the saltshaker back on the table while simultaneously dropping the flashlight into your lap.

What You'll Do

This trick should be done while you're seated at a table.

1. Secretly hold the flashlight in the palm of your left hand.

2. Pick up the saltshaker with your right hand and set it in your fisted left hand. (Fig. A)

3. Give the top of the saltshaker a magic tap, and at the same time squeeze your small flashlight. (Fig. B) This will cause the salt crystals to glow. (Fig. C)

4. When you lift the shaker from your hand, release the flashlight and set the shaker on the table.

5. As you put the saltshaker on the table, drop the flashlight into your lap, disposing of your secret gimmick. (Fig. D)

How to Make Magic with Your Sugar

So your romantic dinner has come to a close. You've paid the bill and offered up the last bite of chocolate mousse to your date. You want to make this a night you'll both remember for the rest of your lives. The violinists have already serenaded, the flower girl has already sold you a rose, but the magic seems to be slipping away—and your date seems to be making eyes at the bartender. Quick! Use a little magic to bring your date's eyes back to you, where they belong!

What They See

You ask your date for a coin and have her initial it with a pen or marker. Your date places the coin on the table and you pick it up. You rub the coin between your hands and—poof!—it's gone. Now you ask your date to select a packet of sugar from the sugar holder. She hands you the packet, and you tear it open. As you pour out the sugar, out drops the initialed coin!

What You'll Need

A coin

A packet of sugar

A date

Fig. A. Ask your date to initial the coin and set it on the table.

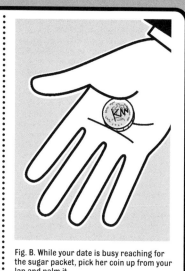

Fig. B. While your date is busy reaching for the sugar packet, pick her coin up from your lap and palm it.

Fig. C. When your date hands you the packet, place it on top of the palmed coin.

Fig. D. Now tear the packet open and pour out the sugar—releasing the coin as you pour!

What You'll Do

There really is not much preparation for this trick. All you need to do is vanish the coin.

1. Have your date choose a coin; ask her to initial it with a pen and place it on the table. (Fig. A)

2. Now, in one swift motion, *pretend* to pick up the coin: With your hand over the coin, palm-side down, slide the coin toward the edge of the table (toward your body) and let it secretly drop into your lap. As your hand reaches the end of the table, close your hand into a fist, giving the illusion that you have the coin in your hand.

3. Rub your hands together and show that you have vanished the coin.

4. Now ask your date to hand you a packet of sugar.

5. As your date reaches for the packet, pick her coin up out of your lap and palm it. (Fig. B)

6. When she hands you the packet of sugar, place it on top of the palmed coin. (Fig. C)

7. Tear the packet open and pour the sugar onto the table, releasing the coin as you pour. (Fig. D)

Sweet success! You've made the coin vanish and reappear in the packet.

How to Make
a Coin Pass Through
an Ashtray

So you just quit smoking—good for you! Not much fun, is it? Especially since your friends all still smoke. And the bar you're in is filled with the stuff. And you have nothing better to do with your hands but wish they had a smoke in them. . . . Well here's a little something that will at least let you make some smoke, without actually smoking! Your friends will think you've been a magician even longer than you were a smoker.

What They See

You cover the top of a clear glass with a small aluminum ashtray, face-up, preventing anything from getting into the glass. You wrap a coin in a small piece of paper. You place the paper in the center of the ashtray and set it on fire. As the paper burns you all hear a *kerplunk*. Lo and behold, the coin has passed through the paper and penetrated the aluminum ashtray.

What You'll Need

A clear drinking glass

Two coins of the same year

An aluminum ashtray

A 4-inch square piece of paper

Fig. A. Place the coin so that it sits in the center of the fold.

Fig. B. Fold each side of the paper into the middle. With the ½-inch overhang folded over, it will appear that the coin is trapped in the paper.

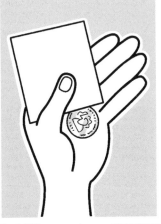

Fig. C. While you search your pocket with your other hand, allow the coin to slip out of the paper and into your hand.

Fig. D. Put the paper on the ashtray and set it aflame. The fire will melt the wax and release the coin into the glass!

Some wax (about the amount you'd get from a small
   birthday candle)
A box of matches or a lighter

What You'll Do

This amazing feat will take a bit of preparation out of sight of your friends.

1. Take one of the coins and adhere it to the bottom of the ashtray using a small amount of melted wax. Now you're ready for your audience.

2. Place the ashtray on top of the drinking glass, face-up.

3. Produce the duplicate coin and ask one of your friends to note the year on the coin.

4. Now fold the coin into the paper as follows so that it can slip into your hand undetected: Fold the paper almost in half, leaving about a ½-inch overhang on the top. Place the coin so that it sits in the center of your fold. (Fig. A) Now fold each side of the paper inward. The ½-inch top edge is folded over, making it appear as though the coin is completely trapped in the paper with no way out. (Fig. B)

5. As you reach to pick up your lighter or matches with your opposite hand, allow the coin to slip out of the paper and into your hand. (Fig. C)

6. Place the paper on the ashtray and set it aflame. (Fig. D) This will cause the wax to melt and allow the coin sticking to the ashtray to drop into the glass. *Kerplunk!*

How to Restore a
Torn Drinking Straw Wrapper

Just about everybody knows how to shoot a straw wrapper off a straw with one strong breath. And just about everybody knows how to make a straw wrapper snake with a little cola. But how many people know how to tear a straw wrapper apart and then put it back together with the help of a little salt? Well, after you finish reading this, you will. This trick is good for at least five minutes of diner fun.

What They See

You pick up a straw and remove the wrapper, keeping the wrapper in one piece. You rip the wrapper in half, then in quarters, then in eighths. Now you roll the eight pieces into a tight ball. You place the ball on the table and request that your friend sprinkle the ball with some salt, just to add a little flavor to your presentation. When your friend unravels the small ball of paper, the wrapper has been restored to its original condition.

What You'll Need

A wrapped straw

An intact straw wrapper

A saltshaker

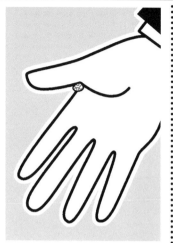

Fig. A. Roll a straw wrapper into a small ball and conceal it at the base of your thumb.

Fig. B. Rip a duplicate wrapper into eight pieces, roll it into a ball, and place it on the table, near the end opposite the saltshaker.

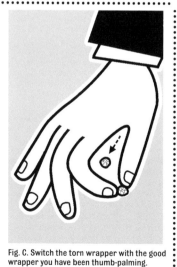

Fig. C. Switch the torn wrapper with the good wrapper you have been thumb-palming.

Fig. D. Have your spectator unravel the ball—it's as good as new!

What You'll Do

This trick requires some advance preparation.

1. At some point before performing the trick, while your friend is either distracted or using the restroom, you must roll a straw wrapper into a small ball and conceal it at the base of your thumb. (Magicians call this a "thumb palm"; it's how they conceal small objects that they later produce from thin air.) (Fig. A)

2. Make sure that the saltshaker is at one end of the table.

3. Once you have your friend's attention, remove the wrapper from a second straw and say, "Did you know that straw wrappers have magical healing powers? Let me show you."

4. Proceed to rip the wrapper into eight pieces and roll them into a tight ball.

5. Place the ball on the table, close to the end far opposite the salt-shaker. (Fig. B)

6. Ask your friend to sprinkle a little salt on the ball.

7. While your friend is reaching for the salt, take the opportunity to switch the torn wrapper with the good wrapper you have been thumb-palming. (Fig. C)

8. After your friend has sprinkled the salt onto the ball, have him unravel the ball. Voilà!—the wrapper is good as new! (Fig. D)

How to Make a Shot Glass Disappear

Everybody loves a free drink. And even more so when they just keep coming! With a little help from a friend, you can pull the shot glass right out from another friend's mouth. And if you do the trick just right, they'll be buying shots all night just to try to figure out how you did it. (*Warning:* If the shots keep coming, be careful. The more drinks, the sloppier the magician.)

What They See

You cover a full shot glass with a handkerchief. You lift the covered glass by the rim and allow several of your companions to reach under the handkerchief to confirm that the glass is still there. You toss the handkerchief high into the air—and the shot glass has completely vanished! Calmly, you reach into your pocket, pull out the shot glass, and drink back your shot.

What You'll Need

Two full shot glasses

A handkerchief

A piece of cardboard the same size as the mouth of a shot glass

Plastic wrap

A rubber band

A jacket

A confederate

Fig. A. Cover the shot glass with your hand-kerchief so that the sewn-in disk lies flat on top of the glass.

Fig. B. Your confederate secretly removes the glass from under the cloth, while you keep your hand around the disk to make it appear that the glass is still there.

Fig. C. Hold the covered glass just above the edge of the table so that your confederate can remove the glass as she reaches under the cloth.

Fig. D. Reach into your pocket, slide the rubber band and plastic off of the glass, and pull out the duplicate glass with a flourish!

What You'll Do

This effect will require a bit more preparation than most of the tricks in this book. (**Note:** This trick works best when you and your friends are seated around a table.)

1. Before you go out to the bar, glue or stitch a disk of cardboard the same size as the mouth of a shot glass into the center of your handkerchief.

2. Once you meet your friends, enlist the help of a confederate, who will assist you in pulling off this feat. Confer with her in advance, and review step 9 below, so that she's prepared to come to your assistance.

3. Order a round of shots for you and your friends.

4. After a suitable interval, excuse yourself to go to the restroom. On the way there, out of sight of your friends, ask the bartender for another shot.

5. Cover this shot glass with the plastic wrap and seal it closed by placing the rubber band around the rim.

6. Now carefully stow this in your jacket pocket.

7. When you return to your seat, the fun can begin. As described in "What They'll See," cover the shot glass with your handkerchief, being careful to place the cloth so that the disk lies flat on top of the glass. (Fig. A) Hold the glass and disk from the top, so that the disk is in your palm and your fingertips hold the walls of the glass.

8. Ask each of your friends seated at the table to reach under the handkerchief to confirm that the glass is still there.

9. Stand up and walk over to your last friend—*your confederate*. She secretly removes the glass as you hold onto the disk, making it appear to your friends that the glass is still there. (Fig. B) This is how it's done: You hold the handkerchief-covered glass just above the table's edge, allowing her to quickly move the glass beneath the table while "confirming" that the glass is still under the cloth. (Fig. C)

10. To further distract the others, quickly move away from the table so that your helper can dispose of the glass undetected.

11. Now toss the handkerchief high into the air. As it falls, snatch it from the air—presto! The glass is gone!

12. But now it gets even better: You reach into your jacket pocket, taking care to slide the rubber band and plastic off of the glass as you do so, then pull out the duplicate glass. (Fig. D) Your friends will be dumbfounded by your extraordinary feat!

How to Make Ouija Board Magic with a Drinking Straw

Has this ever happened to you? You're out on the town and one of your friends suggests that you all go to the street-corner psychic. Next thing you know, you're shelling out 20-dollar bills so that Madame Maria can tell you what you already know (you still haven't found "the one," you'll be rich in another 20 years, and what you really want to do is direct). Here's a way to save your cash by using an ordinary drinking straw to plumb the mysterious psychic powers of the Ouija board.

What They See

You place the straw down on a smooth tabletop and request that everyone concentrate their mental powers on the straw. (You can also use a cigarette, but the surgeon general suggests you use a straw.) You ask one of your friends to ask the Ouija straw a "yes or no" question. If the straw moves to the right side of the table, the answer is "yes." If it moves to the left, the answer is "no." You tell your friends that, if you all concentrate hard enough, you just may be able to make the straw move across the table. In seconds, of its own accord, the straw moves across the table to reveal its answer.

What You'll Need

A drinking straw cut down to about 3 inches

A Swiss army knife or other sharp implement

What You'll Do

1. Snip your drinking straw down to a 3-inch piece (this will make it roll more easily). (Fig. A, inset)

2. Sit at the center of the table, and place the straw on the table so that the two ends point to your right and your left.

3. Have everyone hunker down over the table, focusing all of their mental powers on the straw.

4. Have one of your friends ask a "yes or no" question. Explain that if the straw moves to the left, the answer is "no"; if it moves to the right, it's "yes."

5. Keeping your lips close together, blow a short, silent breath of air across the tabletop so that the straw moves either to the right or left, depending on the answer you choose. Your head should be about 12 inches behind the straw and about 12 inches above it.

Presto—your friend's question has been psychically answered!

Tip: To strengthen this effect, do not blow at the straw right away. Wait about 20 to 30 seconds. To make the effect even more powerful, have a confederate do the blowing, thereby taking suspicion off of you (just make sure that you place the straw so the ends point to the confederate's right and left).

Fig. A. (inset) Snip your drinking straw down to a 3-inch piece to enhance its rolling capability. Your friends will be amazed when the straw "magically" moves across the table!

How to Play the
Matchbox Shell Game

Down on your luck? Need someone to spare some change for a cup of coffee? How about helping a guy out? We've got just the trick for you the next time you find yourself hard up for cash at the local diner. You'll be rolling in the dough with this shell game . . . at least until the old flatfoots come around the corner and put a lid on your grift!

What They See

You show your friends a matchbox by placing it on the table in front of you. With a snap of your fingers and a wave of your hand, you open the box and find a coin inside. You produce two more matchboxes and show that they're empty. You place the boxes on the table, mix them up, and then ask one of your friends to pick the box with the coin. Bet her a dollar that she can't find it. Sure enough, no matter how hard she tries, she can't find the coin!

What You'll Need

Four identical slide matchboxes that are empty

Two coins

A rubber band

A pen

What You'll Do

This trick requires a bit of preparation. For starters, be sure you're wearing a long-sleeved shirt or jacket, and be sure to bring along four identical, empty slide matchboxes.

1. Before your friends arrive on the scene, insert a coin into two of the matchboxes.

2. Mark one of the matchboxes containing a coin with a small ink dot so that you can identify it. (The dot should be in a spot that's visible but inconspicuous.)

3. Fasten the other matchbox containing a coin to your forearm, just above your wrist, with a rubber band. (Fig. A) You have now created a rattle-box. Slip your sleeve over the box so that it's concealed from view.

4. Now you're ready to perform. As described in "What They See," place the marked matchbox on the table, give a magical snap of your fingers, and slide the drawer out to show your spectators the coin.

5. Place the two empty matchboxes on the table (show the audience that they're empty) and shuffle the three boxes around, keeping up your magician's patter all the while. (Fig. B)

6. Ask one of your friends to point to the box with the coin. (Be clear with your directions: Your friend **should not** pick up the box, but only point to it.) (Fig. C)

7. No matter which box your friend picks, you tell her she's wrong: you

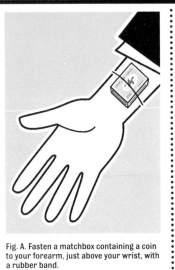

Fig. A. Fasten a matchbox containing a coin to your forearm, just above your wrist, with a rubber band.

Fig. B. Place the two empty matchboxes on the table alongside the other matchbox with the coin, and shuffle the three boxes around.

Fig. C. Ask one of your friends to point to the box she thinks contains the coin.

Fig. D. Prove her wrong by picking up and shaking an empty box, making sure to use the same hand that has the rattle-box attached above it.

prove it by picking up an empty box with the hand that has the rattle-box attached above it and shaking it (in fact, you're really just shaking your rattle-box). (Fig. D)

Example: Say your friend points to the box with the coin. You prove her wrong by picking up one of the empty boxes and rattling the rattle-box—thereby proving that the coin is in the empty box. If your friend points to an empty box, you prove her wrong by picking it up and giving your rattle-box a shake.

Tip: For an added twist, if a child is present, you can make her always right and the adult always wrong.

How to Organize Your Cash with Magic

The local pool sharks are out. They've taken everyone's money but yours. Why? Because you haven't played them yet, and with any luck you won't have to. But suddenly your luck runs out and your name comes up. There's only one way to throw them off guard: the old everyday magician's flashy cash trick. (*Warning:* This trick does not guarantee a pool hall victory, but at least you'll get to have a little fun with your money before it's gone.)

What They See

You remove five one-dollar bills from your pocket. You show them all to be facing in the same direction. One at a time, you place the bills on the pool table, alternately placing one face-down and then the next face-up. You pick up the stack of bills and turn them over. Now the back of the bottom bill should be against the palm of your hand and the top bill should be facing up. But when you display the bills, they are magically all facing up.

What You'll Need

Seven one-dollar bills

Rubber cement

What You'll Do

All you'll need to prepare this trick beforehand is to take four one-dollar bills

Fig. A. Use the rubber cement on the backs of two bills to create a double-faced bill.

Fig. B. Fan out the bills to show your audience that they're all face-up.

Fig. C. Now arrange the regular and gimmick bills so that the stack appears to have been shuffled, with the bills alternating face-up and face-down.

Fig. D. Pick up the bills and flip the entire stack over so that the top bill is face-up. When you fan out the stack, all the bills will be face-up!

and make two gimmick bills out of them.

1. Before you go out for the evening, rubber-cement two bills back-to-back to create a double-faced bill. (Fig. A) Do the same thing with two more bills.

2. Place your bills on the table all facing up. Your two gimmick bills should be in the second and fourth positions.

3. Pick up the stack and fan them to show that they are all face-up. (Fig. B)

4. Remove the top bill and place it on the table face-down (first position).

5. Drop a gimmick bill on top of it (second position) face-up.

6. Place the next bill, which is regular, face-down (third position).

7. Drop another gimmick bill on top of that (fourth position) face-up.

8. Place your last bill face-down (fifth position). The stack now appears to be thoroughly shuffled with the bills alternating face-down, face-up. (Fig. C)

9. Pick up the stack of bills from the table. As you do this, flip the entire stack over so that the top bill of the stack is face-up. (Fig. D)

10. When you fan out the stack, all of the bills will be neatly facing upward.

Tip: Unlike most of the tricks in this book, this is one of the few that can be repeated soon after you've performed it, so long as you're sure that no one wants to examine the bills more carefully the next time. When you repeat the trick, say to your audience, "Watch closely, maybe I went too fast the first time."

How to Make a
Saltshaker Vaporize

Blind date not going so well? You thought she'd like your "retro" leisure suit and tube sock outfit, but she doesn't. You've tried to charm her with your best childhood stories of the time your mom brought a houseful of guests into the bathroom during your tub time, but she just doesn't seem to get it. Why not try a little saltshaker magic? There's no guarantee it'll do the trick, but at this point, what have you got to lose?

What They See

While seated at your favorite restaurant, you announce that you are now going to magically vanish a small object. You borrow a small coin from your dinner date, place the coin on the table, and say: "Let me give you a little history lesson on the topic of salt. Long ago it was used as currency and traded for food and goods. The more salt you had, the richer you were. The Egyptians used it for mummification. Bodies were soaked in a salt solution for as long as 70 days before they were wrapped in cloth. Salt can affect the human body. Not enough salt can cause dehydration and too much salt causes high blood pressure." You cover the borrowed coin with a saltshaker. You cover the saltshaker with a paper napkin. You turn to your date and say, "Let's see how good your memory is. When I placed the coin on the table, was it heads or tails?" You lift the shaker and napkin to reveal the coin. At this point you either congratulate your date on her great memory, or poke some fun at her lousy memory. Then you replace the napkin-covered shaker and have her give it a magic tap with her finger. To her amazement, the saltshaker has completely vanished!

What You'll Need

A paper napkin

A saltshaker

A small borrowed coin

What You'll Do

For this effect, misdirection is everything.

1. As described above, borrow a small coin, place it on the table, then go through your patter about the history of salt.

2. Cover the coin by placing the saltshaker over it.

3. Cover the shaker with a paper napkin.

4. Ask your date to recall whether the coin was heads or tails.

5. When you lift the napkin-covered shaker to reveal heads or tails, bring the shaker to the very edge of the table, toward your body.

6. Let the shaker secretly fall into your lap while you retain the shape of the shaker in the napkin.

7. Once again cover the coin with what your companion thinks is a napkin-covered shaker.

8. Now ask your date to give the shaker a magic tap. To her surprise, there's nothing under the napkin!

9. In one quick motion, bring the shaker from your lap to your pants pocket, and back into view, to give the illusion that you produced the vanished shaker from your pocket.

How to Stick a Knife
Through a Five-Dollar Bill
Without Making a Hole

So, you're being held up at knifepoint and your friendly neighborhood mugger wants all of your money. If you don't know self-defense, give it to him. If you don't know how to act like you don't understand English, give it to him. If you don't know this magic trick, give it to him. But if you've learned this trick well enough, you just might amuse your mugger enough to let you off the hook.

What They See
You fold a five-dollar bill into a folded piece of paper. You push the knife's shank down through the center of the bill, penetrating its paper shell. When you remove the knife, your bill is unharmed.

What You'll Need
A 3 x 5 inch piece of paper

A five-dollar bill

A single-edge razor blade

A knife (a steak knife works well)

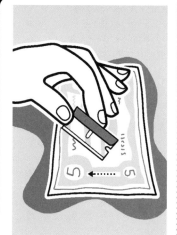

Fig. A. Make a half-inch vertical incision about a quarter inch from the end of the bill.

Fig. B. Place the folded bill into the folded paper so that the two folds meet. (Both the bill and the paper should be folded just about in half, but a little off-center.)

Fig. C. Insert the knife into the slit bill so that the blade bypasses the center of the bill but penetrates the center of the paper shell.

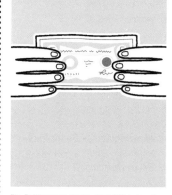

Fig. D. When you display the bill front and back to show that it's unharmed, be sure to hold the bill by both sides, so that your fingers conceal the slit from view.

What You'll Do

You'll need a little preparation for this trick.

1. With a single-edge razor blade, make a half-inch vertical incision about a quarter inch from the end of the bill, halfway between the top and bottom. (Fig. A) The slice will be camouflaged by the bill's design. (This works best with the old-style five-dollar bills.)

2. Cut yourself a 3 x 5-inch piece of paper.

3. Fold the paper in half, but a little off-center, so that the 3-inch edges do not quite meet.

4. Now, in front of your spectator, do the same to your five-dollar bill: Fold it just about in half, but a little off-center.

5. Place the folded bill into the folded paper, so that the two folds meet. The slit end of the bill should be square with the back edge of the paper. (Fig. B)

6. Now insert the knife into the slit so that the blade bypasses the center of the bill but penetrates through the fold of the outer paper shell. Folding the bill off-center has created the illusion that the knife is going into the center of the bill. (Fig. C)

7. Now unfold the bill and display the bill front and back to show that there is no hole. Be sure to hold the bill on both sides, with your thumb and index finger concealing the slit from view. (Fig. D)

What mugger could resist this disarming magical feat?

How to Read
Your Date's Mind

Have you ever been on one of those dates where you just . . . click? Yeah, we haven't either. That's why we're divulging this surefire way to read your date's mind . . . so at least you can make it seem like you've clicked. (**Note:** This trick does not involve asking someone what their favorite color is and then saying, "Mine too!" Although that trick works sometimes, too.)

What They See

You remove a dollar from your pocket. You ask your date to mentally select a single digit from the serial number. As you concentrate and gaze into his eyes, you reveal his thoughts.

What You'll Need

A dollar bill

A pencil

A business card

What You'll Do

This effect is always ready to go and takes little preparation.

1. Beforehand, find a bill in your wallet that has no more than four different numbers in it. (You may have to search a few dozen bills before you

find one that has the right kind of serial number.) For purposes of example, we'll use the serial number 3 8 4 7 3 4 7 8. (You should adjust the numbers in steps 2 through 5 to match the numbers on your bill.) Using a bill like this will make it look as though you're giving your date many choices, but in reality there are only four possible ones.

2. On the left side of the bill, pencil the number "4" on George Washington's forehead.

3. Also on the left side of the bill, under the serial number, write: "All brilliant people think of the number 7."

4. On the back of the bill, write in large letters, "George knew you would select the number 3."

5. And finally, on the back of one of your business cards, write, "I knew you would choose the number 8."

6. Now you're ready to perform. Place the business card face-up on the table between you and your date.

7. Fold the bill in half widthwise, but slightly off-center, so that the writing on George's head is not visible. Show your date the right half of the bill, and ask him to select a single-digit number.

8. With a little showmanship and pizzazz, you're now able to determine his number: Take a look at your bill, choose one of the serial digits, and use it in the following patter:

"If I were truly psychic, I could look into your eyes and say, [your date's name here], you are thinking of the number 8."

If he is thinking of the number 8, you will have totally blown his mind. But if he says, "No, I wasn't thinking of 8," you say, somewhat mysteriously, "Well, okay, I guess I'm not psychic after all—but you know what? George Washington was. What was the number you were thinking of?"

9. At this point the number he reveals will determine your next step. If he says it was the number 4, slightly shift the fold on the bill to reveal that the number 4 is indeed on George's forehead.

10. If he says it was the number 7, flip the bill so that the left side is showing, and show your date where you've written, "All brilliant people think of the number 7."

11. If he says he chose the number 3, reveal the back of the bill to him, where you've written, "George knew you would select the number 3."

12. If he says he chose the number 8, but you did not guess 8 initially (see step 8), flip over your business card, where you've written, "I knew you would choose the number 8."

Tip: Be sure that your business card is sitting on the table face-up so that your date doesn't think you have a business card with each different number written on the back.

Note: This is one of those tricks that should only be performed once. Your audience will be very suspicious the second time around.

How to Use Your X-Ray Vision on a Paper Cup

Okay, so you're no Superman—though for as many burgers as you just ate, your arteries wish you were. Maybe you're a little more Clark Kentish (be sure to take off your glasses for this trick). Either way, they both had X-ray vision, right? The only thing they couldn't see through was a lead object. Fear not, you'll be using a disposable cup for this trick. And since cup makers stopped making disposable cups out of lead back in the 1950s, we think you'll be fine.

What They See

You line the three cups up on the tabletop and wad up a paper napkin into a ball. You turn your back and have your friends place the balled-up napkin under one of the cups. They let you know that they're finished. You turn around to face the cups, gaze at them intently, and then choose the cup with the hidden napkin. Superman would envy your powers!

What You'll Need

Three empty paper cups

A paper napkin

What You'll Do

This little stunt requires no confederates and virtually no advance preparation.

1. Make sure that the three cups each have a seam running down the side (most do).

2. Set up the cups so that all of the seams are facing the same direction.

3. Ball up the napkin, then ask your friends to place the balled-up napkin under one of the cups while your back is turned.

4. By placing the napkin under the selected cup, your friends will change the position of the seam. This will be your clue as to which cup the napkin is under.

5. Turn around and reveal the correct cup.

Tip: Showmanship is important here. Pretend to concentrate as you gaze at the cups. Think really hard and don't be so quick to divulge the selected cup.

Appendix A:
MAGIC ON THE WEB

Ready to learn more about the world of magic? The Web is packed with amazing resources, including newsletters, catalogs, chat groups, and clubs. Here's just a small sampling:

All Magic Guide: www.allmagicguide.com. One of the top magic sites on the Web, with everything from the history of magic, to prop resources, to newsletters, to a guide to televised and live events, and even magic on the radio.

Annie's Magic Shop: www.anniesmagicshop.com. A great site for card tricks, coin tricks, magic books, magic videos, and a variety of magic links.

Diamond Jim: www.diamond-jim.com. Diamond Jim Tyler, a magician and inventor of illusions, here offers a fascinating magic newsletter and his latest magic effects.

International Brotherhood of Magicians: www.magician.org. The home page of the IBM, the world's largest organization of magicians, serving over 15,000 members worldwide. With more than 300 local groups (called "rings") in more than 73 countries, the IBM is the most respected organization for amateur and professional magicians in the world.

Magic Castle: www.magiccastle.com. The Magic Castle is the clubhouse for the Academy of Magical Arts, an organization devoted to the advancement of the ancient art of magic. Located in a turn-of-the-century mansion in the hills above Hollywood, the Castle promotes public interest in the art form, offers classes for professionals and hobbyists, and serves as a unique performance venue. (Be sure to take the virtual tour!)

***Magic* Magazine:** www.magicmagazine.com. Described as the "the independent magazine for magicians," *Magic* magazine offers monthly feature stories, interviews with famous magicians, new tricks, editorials and reviews, and comprehensive performance listings for magic venues far and wide.

Magic Shop: www.magicshop.com. This is the home of Brad Burt, a magician and an inventor of illusions, offering a newsletter and his own special magic effects.

Magic Talk: www.magictalk.com. Magic Talk is the "official discussion group for magicians," moderated by Bryan Dean. Open to all magicians, amateur and professional, Magic Talk provides a forum for magicians seeking to improve their performance skills as well as a nightly chat group.

Magic Times: www.magictimes.com. A magic daily covering the very latest in magic news, including magic press coverage, tour dates, magic-related Web stories, club reports, and more.

McBride Magic: www.mcbridemagic.com. Follow the acts of the great Jeff McBride and many others. This site provides live show listings for all the great magicians performing today. McBride also offers *The Secret Art*, an excellent online journal of magic and magic wisdom.

Philly Magic: www.phillymagic.com. This site is the home of Philadelphia's finest magic shop, Hocus Pocus: a great place to locate unusual magic that you will find nowhere else on the Web. Find the answers to all your magical questions—simply e-mail Irv Furman at info@phillymagic.com.

Society of American Magicians: www.magicsam.com. Billing itself as "the oldest magical society in the world," the SAM is a great place to meet other people interested in magic and learn about magic circles in your area.

True Magic: www.truemagic.com. A great resource for all things Houdini. Here you can read the biography of Harry Houdini, watch the Houdini movie, and take a virtual tour of the Houdini Museum.

Appendix B:

MAGICAL ONE-LINERS

Every magician—whether performing onstage or in any of the every-day situations described in this book—needs to learn the elements of "patter." What is patter? Patter is the steady stream of monologue that magicians use to entertain and distract their audiences as they perform their feats of magic.

Here are some tried-and-true one-liners—some of them real groaners—that are *guaranteed* to amuse and distract! You can use them in your patter while performing any number of the tricks in this book.

Ice Breakers

- Please watch very closely as I do this trick—at no time will my fingers leave my hand!
- I can see that your watch was purchased from a millionaire—his name is J.C. Penney.
- One mind reader said to the other, "You're fine, how am I?"

And now for my next trick . . .

- My next trick was invented by one of the greatest magicians of our time. I've invented others of course, but modesty prevents me from taking credit for them.
- My next trick is actually awfully simple. . . . I've even been told it's simply awful.
- I'm about to perform a miracle—that is, if it works.

- You may ask the question, will he dazzle me with magic or astonish me with his feats of prestidigitation? I really don't know the answer to that question, but you still can ask.
- Don't boo yet, my next trick is even worse.

All About Me

- When I was younger, I wanted to become a comedian but I was afraid everyone would laugh at me.
- If you think these tricks are boring, just think how I feel! I have to put up with them almost every day.
- I have no idea how I do this, and also I have no idea why I do this.
- I don't want you to make a fuss over me, I just want to be treated like any other celebrity.
- Most magicians take years to get their act together. I will attempt to do it right before your eyes.

Timing Is Everything

- I performed this trick in Egypt [pause] . . . I had them rolling in the Nile.
- I've performed this trick for the president [pause] . . . of Local 226.
- I've just signed a big contract [pause] . . . with our local cable television station.

Conversion Chart

Everyday magic can be performed anywhere in the world! Simply use the chart below to magically convert rope lengths, paper sizes, and napkin dimensions into the standard measurements used in your part of the world.

Quantity	Imperial unit	Metric Unit	Imperial to Metric Conversion (approx.)
Length	inch (in)	millimetre (mm) or centimetre (cm)	1 in = 25.4 mm
	foot (ft)	centimetre (cm) or metre (m)	1 ft = 30.5 cm
	yard (yd)	metre (m)	1 yd = 0.914 m

About the Author

During his many years as a magical entertainer, humorist, and educator, Irv Furman has traveled the country, entertaining audiences with his unique style of magic, humor, warmth, and wit. Named by the Society of American Magicians as "the magician's magician," Furman for many years taught a course in magic at Temple University and is the owner of the Hocus Pocus Magic Shop in Philadelphia.